THE GORBALS

—Historical Guide and Heritage Walk—

Caledonia Road Church

Ronald Smith

Other City Council Publications on the City's Heritage
Alexander 'Greek' Thomson - The Glasgow Buildings
Charles Rennie Mackintosh - His Buildings In and Around Glasgow
Queen's Park Historical Guide and Heritage Walk*
Pollokshields Historical Guide and Heritage Walk*
Govan Heritage Trail
Cathcart Heritage Trail
Carmunnock Heritage Trail

*These guides are uniform with this book and available from City Libraries and other retail outlets.

Produced by Development and Regeneration Services, Glasgow City Council, utilising departmental archive material.

Designed and published by Cultural and Leisure Services (Libraries and Archives), Glasgow City Council, Mitchell Library, North Street, Glasgow, G3 7DN.

ISBN 0 906169 56 9

All proceeds from the sale of this publication will be retained by the Council for the production of further guides in this series and for the provision of revised editions.

Foreword

This is a revised, updated and extended version of the first Gorbals Heritage Trail leaflet published by the former City of Glasgow District Council in 1988. As a contribution to the city's celebrations as UK City of Architecture and Design 1999, this guide gives special emphasis to the contrasts between the less than successful redevelopment of the Gorbals in the 1960s and current efforts to achieve long-term success in regeneration.

The first part of the guide provides the historical background to the walk described in the second. In its revised form, it is the third in a new series of local historical guides and heritage walks being produced for interesting parts of Glasgow's south side, the first, Queen's Park and the second, Pollokshields, having been published in 1997 and 1998 respectively.

Because of the Gorbals' proximity to the City Centre, being situated on the opposite (south) bank of the River Clyde, it is readily accessible. Indeed, the Heritage Walk starts and finishes at the suspension footbridge which crosses the river from Clyde Street to Carlton Place.

The route of the Heritage Walk is shown on the map at the end of the book. The main part of the walk is focussed on the Laurieston and central Hutchesontown areas, with options to leave the main route to visit the Southern Necropolis, McNeil Street and the site of the original Gorbals village. Some of the properties described are set back from the public footpath; in these instances, care should be taken to respect the privacy of owners and occupiers.

General information on Glasgow and the Clyde Valley can be obtained from the Tourist Information Centre, situated at Monteith House, 11 George Square, while more detailed local knowledge can be gained from the list of references near the end of this guide.

We hope that you enjoy exploring the Gorbals - one of the best known and fastest changing parts of the city.

Cover photograph:- Looking down the Clyde in the early 1980s, showing part of the Gorbals prior to the current process of regeneration.

Contents

Left:-Crown Street and Hutcheson's Grammar School, September, 1955.

Left:-Aerial photograph looking westwards over the Gorbals, 1996.

THE GORBALS

Introduction

'The Gorbals' is known throughout the world. It is commonly associated with all that was worst in housing conditions and, mainly for that reason, the area was the first in Glasgow to experience wholesale redevelopment after the Second World War. Despite redevelopment, there still remain many reminders of the area's past and these, together with notable modern developments, are the subject of the Heritage Walk in the latter half of this booklet.

The Early History of the Gorbals

The Gorbals, or Brig-end, was originally a single street village which grew up after completion of a bridge, the River Clyde's most westerly crossing point, in 1345 by Bishop Rae of Glasgow. Five years later, a leper hospital dedicated to St. Ninian was founded close to the bridge to cater for plague victims from the City on the opposite bank. After the Reformation, in 1579, the Church feued the lands of the Gorbals to George Elphinstone, a Glasgow merchant. The tower house he built in the village Main Street survived in one form or another until the mid 19th century.

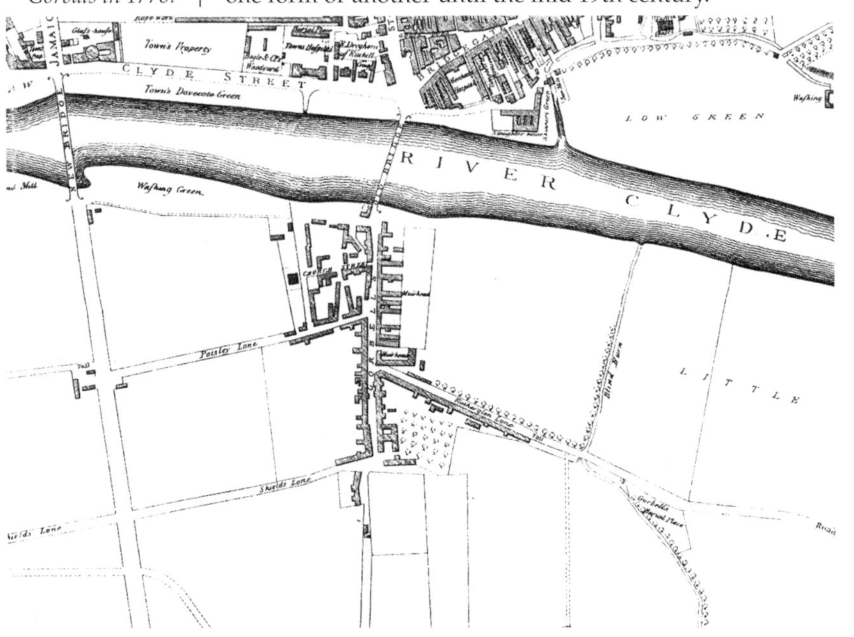

Below:- McArthur's Map showing the Gorbals in 1778.

Early 19th century engraving of Main Street, Gorbals; Elphinstone Tower and St. Ninian's Chapel

Back in the early 17th century, the village of Gorbals was "erected into a Burgh of Barony and Regality" and, in 1650, the magistrates of the City of Glasgow received a Crown Charter to confirm the purchase of the ancient village, together with the lands now occupied by Kingston, Tradeston, Laurieston and Hutchesontown. Around this time, the village is thought to have consisted mainly of thatched houses occupied by maltmen and brewers, but, in 1748, it was extensively damaged by fire.

In 1771, the Parish of Gorbals was created from a very small part of Govan Parish. The new parish, probably the smallest in Scotland, extended to only 14 acres, its boundary drawn tightly around the old village and its burial ground (which, in extended form, still survives as the 'rose garden'). The village's population was 3,500 and it gained 3,000 more inhabitants over the next twenty years.

The City owned the village and surrounding lands in partnership with the Trades' House and Hutcheson's Hospital until 1790 when the area to the west of the line of the present Eglinton Street as far as West Street was transferred to the Trades' House (hence the name Tradeston), the old village was passed to the Town Council and the rest of the area to the east of Eglinton Street became the property of Hutcheson's Hospital.

Towards the end of the eighteenth century, weaving was the village's main industry, with 556 looms in use. There were also gunsmiths, nailers, shoemakers, tailors, wrights and cotton spinners - and no fewer than 60 public houses which, according to the *Old Statistical Account*, "hurt the morals of the people not a little".

In the countryside to the south, the Govan Colliery had been established, tapping three seams of coal and employing over 200 men. The same *Account* records that a steam engine was used to raise coal 600 feet to the surface and considers that "there is such a quantity of coal in the colliery (which belongs to Dunlop and Houston), it would of itself serve the City of Glasgow for a hundred years to come"!

Nineteenth Century Growth and Twentieth Century Decay

Soon after the land transfers, rapid urban growth was initiated, both east and west of the old village. To the east, the patrons of Hutcheson's Hospital promoted the development of Hutchesontown, its original principal streets being Adelphi Street and Hospital Street. Crown Street became the main thoroughfare after the opening of Hutchesontown Bridge (replaced for a second time by the present Albert Bridge). To the west, on ground sold to James Laurie, Laurieston was laid out as a fashionable suburb with broad classical streets mainly named after the English nobility, starting in 1802 with the development of Carlton Place on the riverbank, and followed by "highly genteel" (but now demolished) streets such as Abbotsford Place.

Carlton Place from Clyde Street in 1828.

The continuing Industrial Revolution changed the character of the area with the construction of the Govan Ironworks, better known as Dixon's Blazes, next to the Govan Colliery not far to the south. Buildings and even parts of buildings were demolished to make way for elevated railway lines, carried on stone and brick railway arches. To house the workers in local factories and cotton mills, the rest of the area

was developed throughout the nineteenth century resulting in a remarkably uniform grid-iron layout of four-storey tenements.

The Gorbals lost its administrative independence in 1846 when it was 'annexed' by the City of Glasgow. The village Main Street, including the old Elphinstone Tower, was demolished in the 1870s by the Glasgow City Improvement Trust. A new focal point was created at Gorbals Cross, enhanced by the architecture of Alexander 'Greek' Thomson and eventually by a central clock tower and underground public conveniences!

The Gorbals became a busy place with wide streets, such as Crown Street and Cumberland Street, bustling with commercial activity. Many Glaswegians will recall with some affection the wide straight streets of tenements which once characterised the Gorbals; many former Gorbals residents will remember its warm community spirit. Both memories sharply contradict the 'No Mean City' image of violence which became world famous. In the 1930's, the area was a hive of commercial activity, its 1,000 shops and 130 pubs serving the 90,000 people who lived there. The Gorbals was a true community, assimilating a succession of immigrant groups such as Highlanders, displaced from their homes by sheep, land confiscation and poverty; Irish folk fleeing the famine; Jews displaced by persecution in Europe and Lithuanians displaced by Russians.

Above:-
New tenements under construction at the south-east corner of Gorbals Cross, c.1870, with the remains of St. Ninian's Chapel, then a pub, in the foreground. The Legal Centre now stands on this site (CityArchives).

Right:-
Hutchesontown in the early 1950s, showing St. Francis' Church in the centre (Aerofilms Ltd).

Following pages:-
Map showing the street layout of the Gorbals in 1910. In the 1920s and 1930s, several street names were changed to eliminate duplication of names in the city.

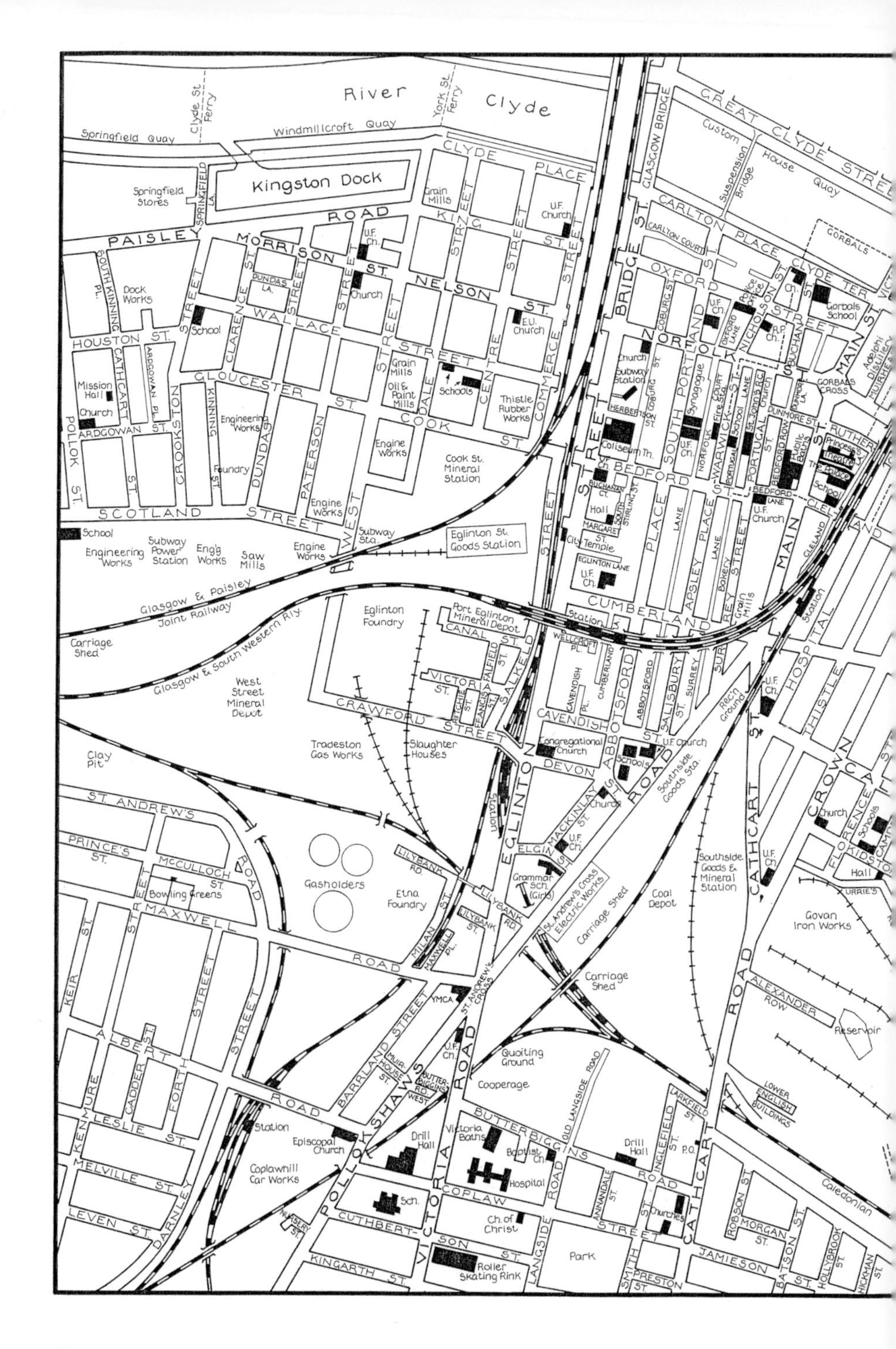
River Clyde
Clyde St. Ferry
York St. Ferry
Springfield Quay
Windmillcroft Quay
Kingston Dock
Springfield Stores
Springfield La.
Paisley Road
Morrison St.
Clyde Place
Great Clyde Street
Custom House Quay
Glasgow Bridge
Suspension Bridge
Carlton Place
Carlton Court
Gorbals
Clyde Ter.
Gorbals School
Grain Mills
U.F. Church
U.F. Ch.
Church
King Street
Nelson St.
E.U. Church
Dock Works
South Kinning Pl.
Houston St.
School
Dundas La.
Wallace Street
Clarence St.
West Street
Centre Street
Commerce Street
Bridge St.
Oxford St.
Coburg St.
Norfolk Street
Nicholson St.
Police Office
R.P. Ch.
Buchan St.
Adelphi Distillery
Gorbals Cross
Main St.
Mission Hall
Cathcart St.
Ardgowan Pl.
Gloucester St.
Kinning St.
Crookston St.
Engineering Works
Grain Mills
Oil & Paint Mills
Dale St.
Schools
Thistle Rubber Works
Subway Station
Herbertson St.
Synagogue
South Portland St.
Fire Sta.
Court
Warwick St.
Lane
St. John's R.C. Church
Dunmore St.
Rutherglen
Princess's Theatre
The Palace
Public Baths
Bedford Row
Bedford Lane
Ardgowan St.
Pollok St.
Foundry
Dundas St.
Paterson St.
Engine Works
Cook St.
Cook St. Mineral Station
Coliseum Th.
Bedford St.
Buchanan Ct.
Hall
Margaret St.
South Stirling St.
City Temple
Scotland Street
School
Engineering Works
Subway Power Station
Eng'g Works
Saw Mills
Subway Sta.
Eglinton St. Goods Station
Eglinton Lane
Place
Apsley Place
Bakery
Surrey Street
Grain Mills
Cleland
Station
Cumberland St.
Glasgow & Paisley Joint Railway
Glasgow & South Western Rly.
Carriage Shed
Eglinton Foundry
Port Eglinton Mineral Depot
Canal St.
Wellcroft Pl.
Cavendish Pl.
Cumberland
Abbotsford
Salisbury St.
West Street Mineral Depot
Victoria St.
Falfield St.
Salkeld St.
Crawford Street
Cavendish St.
Hospital Street
Thistle St.
Rec'n Ground
Congregational Church
U.F. Church
Schools
Devon St.
Abbotsford Pl.
Clay Pit
Tradeston Gas Works
Slaughter Houses
Eglinton St.
Southside Goods Sta.
Crown St.
Church
Florence St.
Schools
St. Andrew's Road
Prince's St.
McCulloch St.
Gasholders
Lilybank Rd.
Mackinlay St.
Elgin St.
Grammar Sch. (Girls)
St. Andrew's Cross Electric Works
Carriage Shed
Southside Goods & Mineral Station
Coal Depot
Cathcart Road
Hall
Govan Iron Works
Bowling Greens
Maxwell Road
Etna Foundry
Milan St.
Maxwell Pl.
Lilybank St.
Carriage Shed
Alexander Row
Reservoir
Keir St.
Albert Road
Forth Street
YMCA
St. Andrew's Cross
Barrland Street
Muirhouse St.
U.F. Ch.
Quoiting Ground
Cooperage
Old Langside Road
Lower English Buildings
Kenmure St.
Cadder St.
Leslie St.
Station
Episcopal Church
Pollokshaws Road
Butterbiggins Rd. West
Drill Hall
Victoria Baths
Butterbiggins Road
Baptist Ch.
Drill Hall
Inglefield St.
Larkfield St.
P.O.
Caledonian
Melville St.
Coplawhill Car Works
Darnley St.
Sch.
Coplaw Street
Hospital
Annandale St.
Churches
Robson St.
Morgan St.
Leven St.
Nursery St.
Cuthbertson St.
Ch. of Christ
Langside Road
Park
Smith St.
Jamieson St.
Batson St.
Hollybrook St.
Hickman St.
Kingarth St.
Victoria Road
Roller Skating Rink
Preston St.

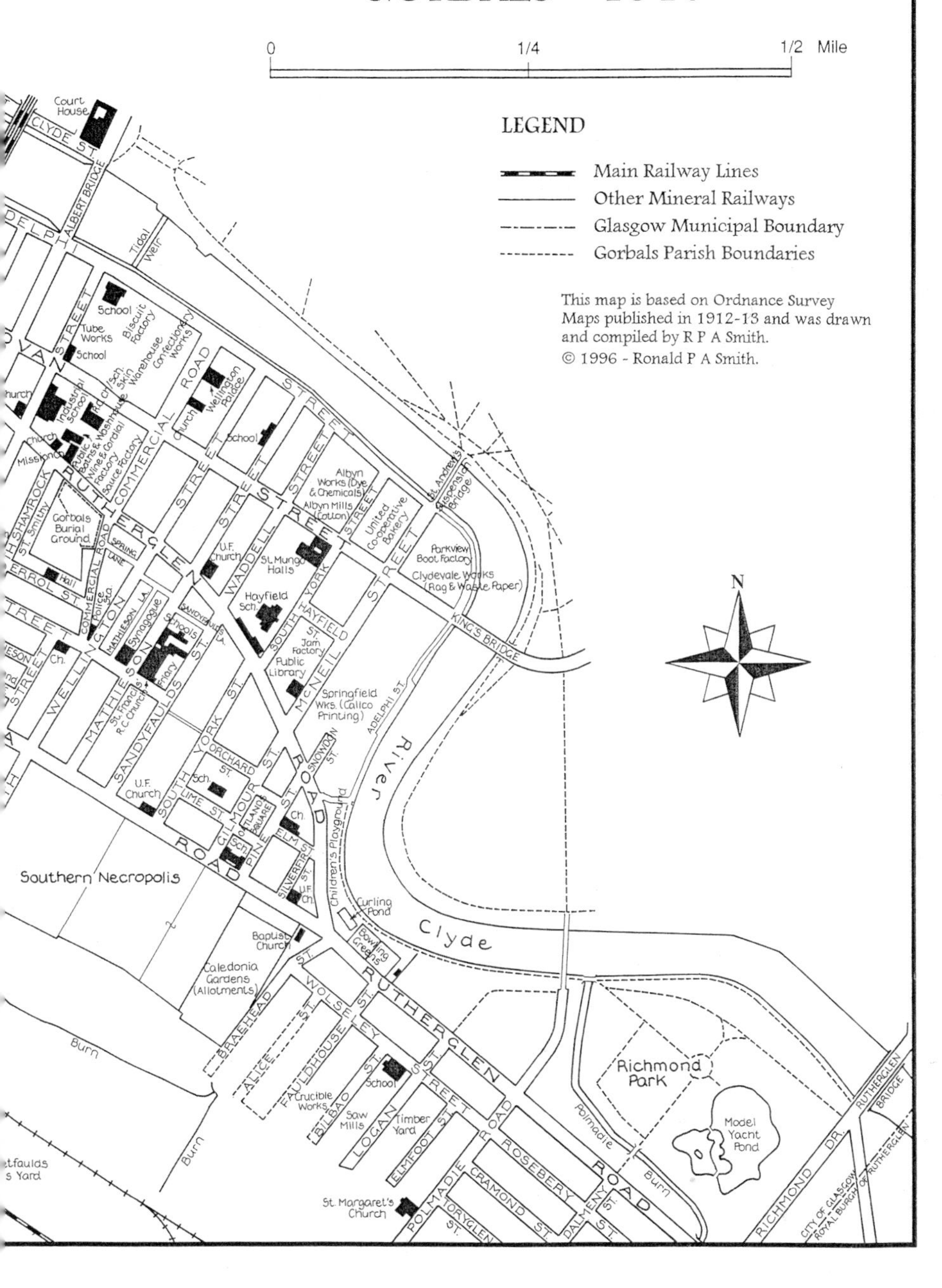
GORBALS ~ 1910
0
1/4
1/2 Mile
LEGEND
Main Railway Lines
Other Mineral Railways
Glasgow Municipal Boundary
Gorbals Parish Boundaries
This map is based on Ordnance Survey Maps published in 1912-13 and was drawn and compiled by R P A Smith.
© 1996 - Ronald P A Smith.
N
Court House
CLYDE ST.
ALBERT BRIDGE
Tidal Weir
School
Tube Works
School
Biscuit Factory
Skin Warehouse
Confectionery Works
Industrial School
R.C. Ch. Sch.
Wash House
Public Baths & Washhouse
Wine & Cordial Factory
Sauce Factory
Church
Mission
Wellington Palace
Church
School
COMMERCIAL ROAD
Gorbals Burial Ground
ST. Smithy
SPRING LANE
Hall
Police Sta.
ERROL ST.
MATHIESON LA.
Synagogue
Schools
Friary
St. Francis' R.C. Church
WELLINGTON
MATHIESON
SANDYFAULDS
SANDYFAULDS ST.
Ch.
U.F. Church
St. Mungo Halls
Hayfield Sch.
WADDELL STREET
SOUTH YORK
HAYFIELD
ST. Jam Factory
Public Library
McNEIL STREET
Albyn Works (Dye & Chemicals)
Albyn Mills (Cotton)
United Co-operative Bakery
St. Andrew's Suspension Bridge
Parkview Boot Factory
Clydevale Works (Rag & Waste Paper)
KING'S BRIDGE
Springfield Wks. (Calico Printing)
ADELPHI ST.
River
Clyde
SNOWDON ST.
ORCHARD ST.
SOUTH YORK ST.
Sch.
LIME ST.
U.F. Church
GILMOUR ST.
PORTLAND SQUARE
PINE ST.
ELM ST.
Ch.
Sch.
SILVERFIR ST.
U.F. Ch.
Children's Playground
Curling Pond
Bowling Greens
Southern Necropolis
ROAD
Baptist Church
Caledonia Gardens (Allotments)
BRAEHEAD ST.
WOLSELEY ST.
ALICE ST.
FAULDHOUSE ST.
RUTHERGLEN
Crucible Works
BILBAO ST.
School
Saw Mills
Timber Yard
LOGAN STREET
ELMFOOT ST.
ROSEBERY ST.
St. Margaret's Church
POLMADIE ROAD
CRAMOND ST.
TORYGLEN ST.
DALMENY ST.
Polmadie Burn
Burn
Burn
Burn
Richmond Park
Model Yacht Pond
RICHMOND DR.
RUTHERGLEN BRIDGE
CITY OF GLASGOW ROYAL BURGH OF RUTHERGLEN
tfaulds s Yard

POLICE

E·SMYTH
PARAGON

Opposite, above:-The west end of Cumberland Street in the 1960s, looking east towards Hutchesontown (and the new multi-storey blocks of Queen Elizabeth Square). The faded grandeur of Laurieston's classical architecture is apparent.

But decay soon set in and, in common with many other inner city areas throughout Britain, this became apparent in the inter-war period. Little was done to address localised problems of building decay, overcrowding or poor sanitation, with the result that the deterioration in conditions became widespread throughout the Gorbals.

A general desire after the Second World War to build afresh was reflected in Government legislation to enable the comprehensive redevelopment of large tracts of cities and towns. In the spirit of the times, and in response to the City's immense housing problems, Glasgow Corporation embarked on an extremely ambitious redevelopment programme involving the designation of 29 Comprehensive Development Areas (CDAs), of which Hutchesontown/Part Gorbals was to be the first.

The High-Rise Solution to Glasgow's Housing Problem and its Impact on Gorbals

In the early 1950's, it was estimated that 600,000 people out of Glasgow's population of 1,085,000 required rehousing - a massive problem calling for imaginative solutions. Because of the need to reduce excessive population densities, only 250,000 (or less than half) could reasonably be accommodated in redevelopment areas within the City boundaries.

The new peripheral estates of Castlemilk, Drumchapel and Easterhouse could house only 100,000 people, and further opportunities for City expansion were severely limited by topography and the imposition of the 'Green Belt' to combat urban sprawl. The remaining 250,000 were expected to move beyond the Green Belt to the New Towns - initially East Kilbride and Glenrothes, but later Cumbernauld, Livingston and Irvine - or to other parts of Scotland where they would be housed through 'overspill agreements' with receiving local authorities as far afield as Arbroath, Wick and Stranraer. The overall planning strategy for the Glasgow conurbation was presented in the Clyde Valley Regional Plan which was released in interim form in 1946 and fully published in 1949.

Opposite, below:-The east end of Cumberland Street in September, 1955 with the Paragon Cinema (a converted church) and St. Francis' Church on the left.

It was estimated that renewal of the City's redevelopment areas with two-storey housing would have accommodated only 75,000 people; four-storey development to modern standards of amenity would have housed twice as many. But to achieve the goal of rehousing 250,000 in these areas, the extra expense of high-rise building was considered justifiable. In any case, the Housing Department of Glasgow

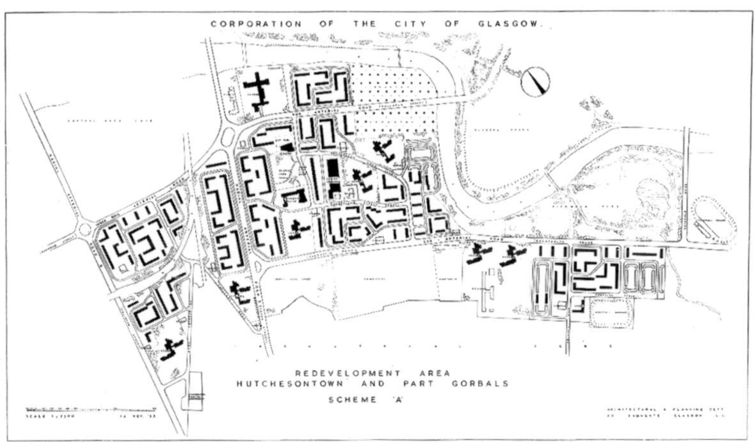

Above and Left:- Early plan and model for the comprehensive redevelopment of Gorbals, stretching from Laurieston (on the left) to Oatlands. The plan is dated November, 1953.

Corporation had been keen to experiment with multi-storey construction for many years, the prototype eight-storey block having been built at Partick (Crathie Court, Laurel Street) over the years 1949-52.

By 1953, Corporation architects had produced sketches to illustrate the possible appearance of proposed tower blocks for the Gorbals, together with a detailed layout plan and model to give some idea of how almost the whole area could be redeveloped. These plans, related to a report approved by the Corporation in November 1953, were put on show at the Modern Homes Exhibition at the Kelvin Hall in 1954. Their approach was, however, more radical and idealised than subsequent circumstances allowed. In practice, the redevelopment of the area was to be tackled in three parts - the Hutchesontown/Part Gorbals Comprehensive Development Area (CDA) (approved by the Secretary of State for Scotland in 1957), the Laurieston/Gorbals CDA (approved in 1966), and an outline CDA for the Oatlands area (which was never implemented).

This striking representation of high-rise living was produced by City architects in 1953.

Hutchesontown/Part Gorbals Comprehensive Development Area

The area's reputation for bad housing conditions was largely borne out by detailed survey work in Hutchesontown, carried out in advance of the redevelopment. Residential property, some of it not particularly old, was generally in poor condition, both from a structural and a sanitary point of view, resulting from neglect by private landlords. The system of factoring had broken down, and thirty years of rent control and lack of investment had taken their toll. Although maintenance was not carried out, the landlords had, in many cases, subdivided the flats, resulting in overcrowding. By 1955, 87% of the flats in Hutchesontown had only one or two rooms and one third were 'back-to-back'.

Looking south in the back court of the street block bounded by Rutherglen Road, Lawmoor Street, Ballater Street and Mathieson Street, September 1955.

The high occupancy of such small dwellings resulted in an average population density of 458.6 persons per acre - compare this to a modern 'suburban' density of 30 persons per acre.

Not only was there a lack of living space, but only 3% of the houses had a bath, and less than a quarter had their own internal WC. Over Hutchesontown as a whole, there was only one toilet for every three houses; often these were provided in brick-built extensions added to stair landings at the back of the tenements. These brick extensions had themselves replaced common lavatories (dry closets) in back court outhouses. Overall, the neglect, the overcrowding and the lack of sanitary facilities added up to the contemporary portrayal as a 'grim picture of living', only partly mitigated by tenants' own internal home-making.

Back courts were also in particularly poor condition, lacking vegetation and characterised by well-trodden earth and ruinous boundary walls and outbuildings, including disused air-raid shelters. Many back courts had been partly or wholly occupied by small industries and commercial premises. In central Hutchesontown, these included an upholsterer's workshop, a grease manufacturing plant, fish curing works and a rag sorting and storage workshop, all in close proximity to dwellings.

Left:-Child dwarfed by the enormity of dilapidation in this 1955 study of a back court at Gilmour Street.

These were some of the more extreme examples, but the sheer mixture and variety which characterised the area ran counter to the post-war planning principle of 'zoning' and the separation of 'land uses' (such as residential, commercial, industrial, open space) into clearly defined areas. The grid-iron street layout was considered undesirable as it encouraged through traffic and because the numerous crossroads were termed accident blackspots. There was a lack of green open space, particularly for schoolchildren.

In summary, the CDA 'Written Statement' said that it was "the opinion of the (Glasgow) Corporation that the area (was) one of bad layout and obsolete development, and that the only satisfactory way of dealing with it (was) to define it as an area of Comprehensive Development under the Town and Country Planning (Scotland) Act, 1947".

Although the fashion of the time was for complete redevelopment, there was some recognition that property could have been saved and refurbished. Ninian Johnston, writing for an architectural magazine in 1957, acknowledged that many of the old buildings had been substantially built to sound individual designs which, but for want of proper maintenance, could have been retained. The area had great appeal, which he described in the following terms:-

"The broad streets, flanked with their uncompromising cliffs of classical tenements diminishing into the distance, have an air of dilapidated, littered grandeur. Slums are generally mean, with nothing in their favour, but here, in parts, is a sort of stricken elegance."

Tenements diminishing into the distance, Lawmoor Street, July 1947.

How the 1950s planners envisaged the completed Hutchesontown redevelopment, prior to alteration and refinement of the layout. Note in particular the contrast with the previous grid-iron pattern of streets (Aerofilms Ltd).

Readers may reach their own conclusions from the photographic evidence available - and it might well be the case that, had the old Gorbals still been with us today, an entirely different approach to the future planning of the area would have been adopted. But acceptance of the concept of large-scale tenement refurbishment had to await the failure of much post-war redevelopment.

Glasgow Corporation completed its detailed survey of Hutchesontown and published the Comprehensive Development Area (CDA) Plan in 1956. The Plan's proposals were scrutinised at a public inquiry and, on 8th February 1957, they were finally approved by the Secretary of State for Scotland.

This CDA, the centrepiece of which was eventually to be the Queen Elizabeth Square high-rise blocks, was intended to house only 10,000 inhabitants, compared to the previous population of 27,000. Despite this, it was envisaged from the outset that half of the houses would be in blocks of about twenty storeys. The estimated cost of the redevelopment was £12,915,000, including acquisition costs of £1,250,000 and demolition expenditure of £500,000.

Hutchesontown 'Area A' (Ballater Place), as new.

The CDA was divided into five principal development areas:-

Area A

This pilot scheme of 96 dwellings in three and four storey blocks at Ballater Place/Commercial Road was completed in 1958 and designed by the City Architectural and Planning Department. The development gained a Saltire Award for good design and, in the early days, the play equipment on the site drew children from far and near.

Area B

In this development of 429 houses at Waddell Court/ Commercial Court (between Ballater Street and the River Clyde, often referred to as 'Riverside'), 308 flats were provided in four 17-storey blocks, the remainder in three and four storey blocks. The north-south orientation of the high-rise blocks, which set the pattern for all such later development throughout the Gorbals, was at variance to the original street layout. The scheme was designed to also include a nursery school, five shops, a community room and two pubs. The architects were Robert Matthew, Johnson-Marshall & Partners and the development was completed in 1964.

Right:-The newly completed Hutchesontown 'Area B' after dark (Jim Mackintosh Photography).

Below:- Hutchesontown 'Areas B and C' under construction, as viewed from Glasgow Green (Jim Mackintosh Photography).

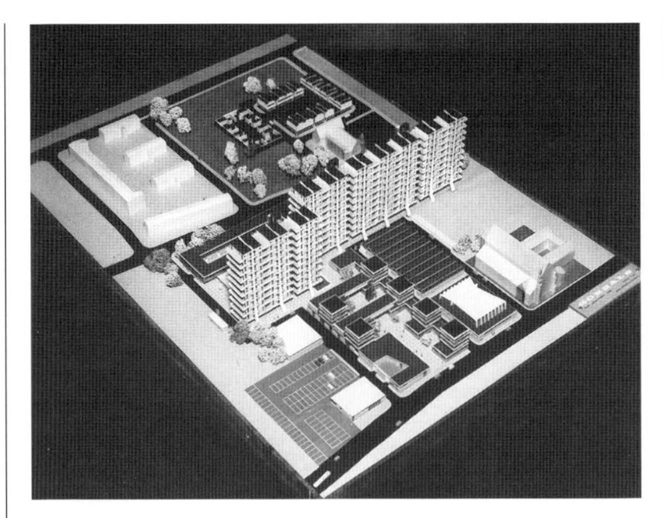

Right:-Model of the proposed high-rise blocks at Queen Elizabeth Square, showing associated industrial units (in the backbround) and car parking, shopping centre and bowling alley (in the foreground).

Area C

The dominant feature of this centrally-located site was the 400 flats and maisonettes in the 20-storey slab blocks known as numbers 2, 16 and 32 Queen Elizabeth Square (as was usual practice in Glasgow, the blocks were not given their own names). At the foot of these blocks was the main shopping centre for the Gorbals community, some of the shop units facing the flats and the rest forming the Cumberland Arcade. The centre provided 26,000 square feet of retail floorspace in the form of 37 shop units of different sizes and one supermarket; also three pubs, offices, two banks and a

Left:-Sir Basil Spence's multi-storey blocks at Queen Elizabeth Square under construction (Jim Mackintosh Photography).

Right:-Cumberland Arcade, with the Queen Elizabeth blocks towering above, 1984.

post office. Above the arcade were another 42 maisonettes while, to the north of Old Rutherglen Road, there was built a still-surviving (but soon to be demolished) 'service trades' development consisting of a two-storey factory block and an open yard. The architects were Sir Basil Spence, Glover & Ferguson. The high flats were completed in 1965 and the shopping centre three years later. Proposals for a cinema, a bowling alley and a multi-storey car park never came to fruition; the site for the bowling alley was used instead to build the John Mains Community Centre.

Left:-Queen Elizabeth Square, looking west, 1984. The shops defining the edges of the 'square' were dwarfed by the tower blocks in the centre!

Below:-The completed Queen Elizabeth flats in 1965, with St. Francis' Church, School and Friary in the foreground. Work on the associated shopping centre at Cumberland Arcade had not yet begun at that stage (Jim Mackintosh Photography).

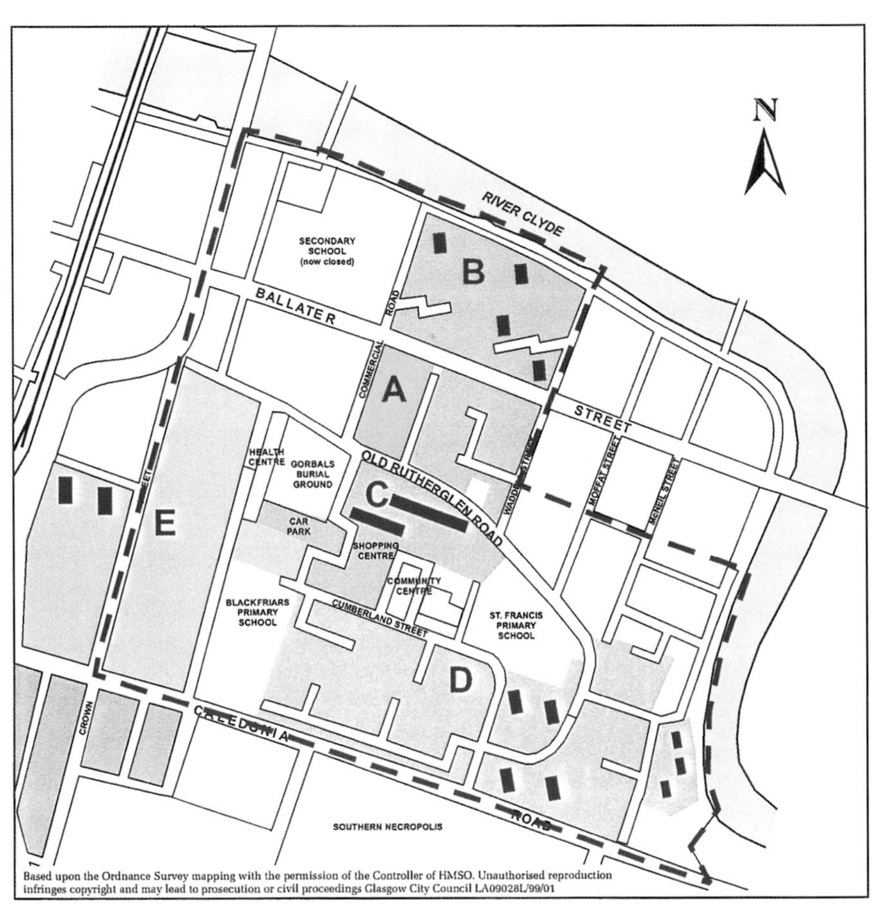

HUTCHESONTOWN/ PART GORBALS COMPREHENSIVE DEVELOPMENT AREA

- Boundary of C.D.A.
- Hutchesontown "Area A", completed 1958 (Glasgow Corporation)
- Hutchesontown "Area B", completed 1964 (Robert Matthew, Johnson-Marshall & Partners for Glasgow Corporation)
- Hutchesontown "Area C", completed 1965-68 (Sir Basil Spence, Glover & Ferguson for Glasgow Corporation)
- Hutchesontown "Area D", completed 1971 (Scottish Special Housing Association)
- Hutchesontown "Area E", completed 1974 (Gilbert Ash for Glasgow Corporation)
- Multi-storey blocks
- C.D.A. Proposals never implemented

The Caledonia Road frontage of Hutchesontown 'Area D' in September 1985, prior to more recent refurbishment work.

Area D

On the large site extending south to Caledonia Road, 1115 flats and maisonettes were developed over the period 1966-71 by the Scottish Special Housing Association (now incorporated into Scottish Homes). 552 of the houses were contained in four 24-storey blocks, and 467 were in four-storey "walk-up" tenemental property, arranged round hard-surfaced pedestrian courts, somewhat fancifully described as "on the Georgian pattern" by Harold Buteux, the SSHA's Chief Technical Officer. Three further eight-storey blocks, much more squat in apprearance and containing a total of 96 flats, were built on the riverfront at Silverfir Court.

Area E

To the west, straddling Crown Street, 1143 system-built 'package deal' houses were constructed by Gilbert Ash Ltd. (part of the Bovis Group) over the period 1969-74, consisting of 384 flats contained in two 24-storey blocks and 759 flats and maisonettes in the now-demolished seven-storey deck-access blocks. All of these buildings were constructed in the 'Tracoba' system of industrialised building (for which Gilbert Ash were the sole UK licencees). The precast units were manufactured by the company at Dalmarnock and transported the two miles to Gorbals on specially prepared trailers. As described later, the seven-storey blocks have had to be demolished because of severe dampness problems and their site is now being developed once again by the Crown Street Regeneration Project.

Hutchesontown 'Area E', looking westwards from the front of Blackfriars School, 1985 and showing both the multi-storey and (then derelict) deck access housing.

An optimistic portrait of the City of Glasgow, published in the Scottish Field in 1964, reflected that "it (was) fitting that some of Scotland's most brilliant architects should have been brought in as consultants. Here (was) the opportunity of pure gold to set the standard". Sir Basil Spence, personally presenting his firm's proposals for Queen Elizabeth Square (Hutchesontown 'Area C') to councillors and officials of Glasgow Corporation, compared the two-storey high level balconies to tenement back greens and said that, on wash day, the effect would resemble "a great ship in full sail". Such was the prestige of the project that Her Majesty the Queen laid the foundation stone and gave her name to the development.

Architects and planners of the time (or some of them at least!) revelled in the Spence blocks' technical achievements and the break from traditional urban form that they represented. They received a Saltire Society Housing Design Award. The first residents appreciated the interiors of the houses, including the modern bathrooms, and liked the views from the windows. But others not so directly connected with this or similar urban housing projects were rather more dubious. The dark, windswept spaces between the curving concrete stilts or piloti holding up the buildings could only be described as a brutal environment, far removed from the conventional character of a 'square'. Here, elderly people (unless well weighed down with shopping) and young

One of the gloomy access corridors in the Queen Elizabeth Square multi-storey blocks.

children frequently had to be helped against the force of the wind. The only relief to board-marked concrete and pebble aggregate was a central water feature - but that was short-lived. Once the novelty had worn off, residents saw the long, dark spinal corridors as an inadequate substitute for the traditional 'street'.

Untroubled by such criticisms, progress on the redevelopment of Hutchesontown had been rapid in the initial stages. By 1964, 16,000 out of the original 27,000 residents had been rehoused. But attention to detail and maintenance, apparent in these early years, became less intensive as interest in the 'showpiece' waned. The Corporation's final housing project in Hutchesontown, the ill-fated 'Area E', although officially 'opened' by the Queen in 1972, was never completed as intended.

We now have the benefit of hindsight; but before going on to consider the redevelopment of Laurieston, it is worth recalling the spirit of the times, again as recorded in the Scottish Field in March 1964:-

"In a quarter of a century, the old Gorbals will be nothing more than a fading memory. Rotting tenements, crowded single-ends, noisome back courts, ill-lit alleyways - all will have gone. In their stead will be not just the blocks and clusters of high flats that are already such familiar landmarks, but spacious schools and playgrounds, rented unit factories, an entertainment building, a new commercial centre - welded by landscaping into a new environment bearing no least resemblance to the old".

TALKING OF BUSTLE... *how's this for the town that is accused of being unable to get off its knees*

JUST a few blocks away the first of the Gorbals giants reach for the sky.

But Glasgow can't wait. Another £7,000,000 development is in the order books. If it's going to be done why not NOW. So the demolishers move into Lawmoor Street just a few weeks after the plan has been approved. Block after block is stripped then disappears in a cloud of dust.

Soon Lawmoor Street itself will vanish —the planners have no use for it in a multi-million-pound housing paradise.

—Picture by STEWART FAIR

From the 'Evening Citizen', March 1962: "Just a few blocks away the first of the Gorbals giants reach for the sky. But Glasgow can't wait. Another £7,000,000 development is in the order books. If it's going to be done why not NOW. So the demolishers move into Lawmoor Street just a few weeks after the plan has been approved. Block after block is stripped then disappears in a cloud of dust. Soon Lawmoor Street itself will vanish - the planners have no use for it in a multi-million-pound housing paradise."

Laurieston/Gorbals Comprehensive Development Area

The Laurieston/Gorbals CDA extended the redevelopment of Gorbals westwards as far as Eglinton Street/Bridge Street and southwards to Eglinton Toll. Glasgow Corporation's reasons for redeveloping the area, as stated in the CDA Survey Report, were summarised as follows:-

"**1.** The area is one of vacant sites, sub-standard, and obsolescent property in which the condition of the existing housing is deteriorating rapidly. The widespread blight thus produced can only be overcome by redevelopment on comprehensive lines;

2. The mixture of the uses and the bad layout in the area militates against the interest and convenience of the land-users concerned and relief depends upon comprehensive redevelopment involving relocation of population, commerce and industry; and

3. The radical changes in road pattern required to meet present and future traffic needs offer the opportunity to reconcile the conflict of interests between the vehicle and the pedestrian."

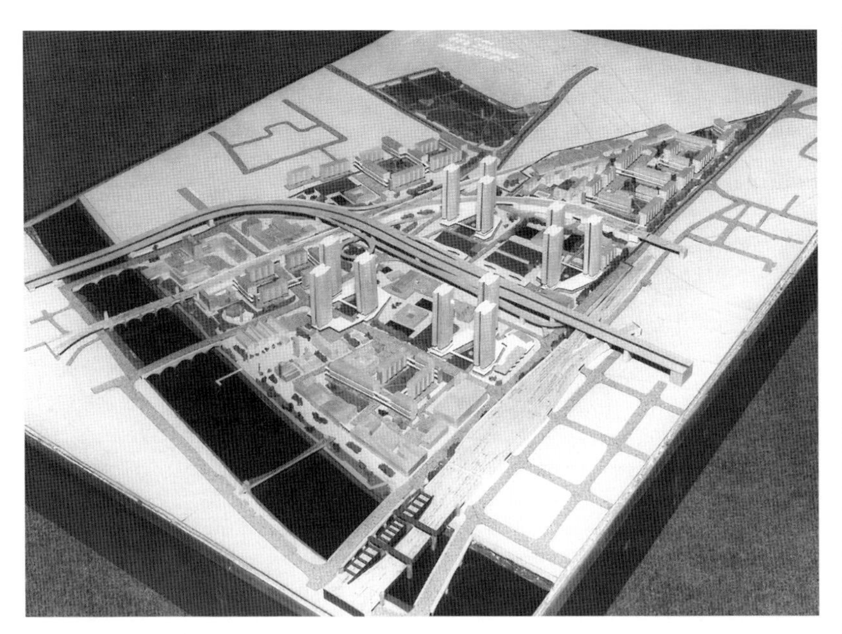

Model showing proposals for the Laurieston/ Gorbals CDA, prominently featuring the south flank of the city's Inner Ring Road (Jim Mackintosh Photography).

Aerial photograph looking north over Laurieston towards the city centre, 1962. Note the flats under construction at Pollokshaws Road and the demolitions that had taken place well in advance of approval for comprehensive redevelopment (Aerofilms Ltd).

The deterioration in the condition of dwellinghouses and the removal of families to new housing estates over the period 1931-1961 had halved the population of Laurieston. The fall in population was further accelerated by considerable piecemeal demolition of tenements which were said to have reached the end of their 'physical life'.

Also, the Corporation's proposals for the city's Inner Ring Road, approved on 29th November 1962, had to be accommodated in the CDA Plan (hence the reference above to radical changes in road pattern). The CDA Survey Report stated that "within the area under review, the Inner Ring Road will sweep in a wide arc from Crown Street at Ballater Street across to Eglinton Street at Bedford Street with connections to and from Gorbals Street and Eglinton Street, and an off ramp to Hospital Street, which will replace Crown Street as a principal arterial road and will eventually be improved to expressway standard as will those parts of Gorbals Street, Eglinton Street and Cathcart Road to the south of the Inner Ring Road. Completely elevated throughout this section, the Inner Ring Road varies in height from 27 feet above ground level at its lowest point to over 45 feet where it passes over the two railway viaducts leading into Central and St Enoch Stations."

Thus the proposed Inner Ring Road was one of the chief reasons for the demolition of the high quality classical tenements in the northern half of Abbotsford Place and the southern half of Nicholson Street. But housing conditions were poor, though markedly better than in Hutchesontown. 99% of the 5571 houses in Laurieston were said to be in the three lowest categories of structural condition, while 62% were considered incapable of satisfactory improvement. 49% contained only one or two apartments; 31% were of the back-to-back type, 30% had shared water closets and only 11% had baths and hot water. During the years 1964-65, 970 houses had been cleared by Glasgow Corporation's Medical Officer of Health under the Housing Acts.

Overcrowding was widespread, 13.4% of dwellings having more than two persons per habitable room. The problem was most apparent in sub-let properties in Abbotsford Place, Nicholson Street and South Portland Street. A subdivided flat in Laurieston might mean an original house of five or six habitable rooms, with bathroom, W.C. and kitchen being let to six or seven families, all sharing the same sanitary and kitchen facilities. The sub-tenant who lived in the kitchen was in a relatively strong position because whoever had the kitchen controlled water supplies, fuel (coal bunkers were usually in the kitchen) and the pulleys for drying clothes. In many cases, the occupant of the kitchen was a kind of factor for the landlord, collecting the rent for the whole house and charging for the use of the coal-fired cooking range.

On the other hand, 54.7% of dwellings had less than one person per habitable room! The housing density was around 120 dwellings per acre. Excluding the riverside garden at Carlton Place, there was only 0.34 acre of public open space, representing 0.02 acre per 1,000 persons.

345 industrial firms occupied 429 premises - a total of approximately 1,350,000 square feet of floorspace employing about 3,850 people. In the vicinity of Gorbals Cross, according to the CDA Survey Report, there were "two groups of interdependent wholesalers - textiles/drapery and fancy goods/smallware". These and other firms tended to occupy converted tenement property.

The 'visionary' architecture of the redeveloped Hutchesontown was not to be repeated in Laurieston. The initial four housing developments were all designed and built by Crudens Ltd.:-

Three illustrations from the 'Highway Plan for Glasgow', 1965.

Upper:-View eastwards along the Inner Ring Road through Laurieston. "This elevated section of motorway will provide many new and exciting glimpses of the City skyline."

Middle:-Looking southwards down Eglinton Street in the vicinity of Bedford Street, with the motorway passing overhead. "Tree and shrub planting from the river southward adjacent to the railway viaduct will produce a 'parkway' effect, greatly improving the amenity of this section of the City."

Lower:-View of pedestrian walkway under the motorway at Laurieston. "This is a typical example of how a motorway can be integrated with new development, by treating the differing architectural forms and landscaping as a whole."

The massive multi-storey blocks of Laurieston Area 1A (Stirlingfauld Place), with the Laurieston Playbarn or Youth Centre in the foreground.

Area 1A (Stirlingfauld Place)

552 flats in two huge 24-storey blocks, completed in 1973. The type of construction was relatively 'traditional', consisting of a concrete frame with roughcast brick infill curtain walls. The sheer scale of these buildings, each two tower blocks in one, makes them overbearing and unappealing from a townscape point of view.

Area 1B (Wellcroft Place/Cavendish Place)

128 flats in 4-storey 'walk up' blocks, also completed in 1973. Their design was loosely based on the 'Scottish vernacular' style with white roughcast, pitched roofs and broad cement bands round some of the windows.

Area 2A (Eglinton Court)

116 flats in the same type of 4-storey blocks as Area 1B, completed in 1974.

Area 2B - (Norfolk Court)

552 flats in two more or less identical 24-storey blocks as in Area 1A, completed in 1976, and therefore some of the last multi-storey housing built in Scotland. These blocks overshadow Gorbals Cross which has, as a result, been transformed from a busy commercial/community focal point to an impersonal, windswept traffic junction.

A further 280 flats in 4-storey walk up blocks were planned for 'Areas 3 and 5', extending southwards from

Cavendish Street to Turriff Street, but these were never built, and interest in completing the redevelopment of the area seemed to tail off. It was not until the early 1980s that the Scottish Special Housing Association (now Scottish Homes) developed the site bounded by Cavendish Street, Abbotsford Place, Devon Street and Eglinton Street. This development was the first in the Gorbals to include two-storey terraced houses with gardens and sheltered housing for the elderly (although 84 'pensioner flats' had previously been provided at Ballater Place/Hutchesontown 'Area A' and at Braehead Street, the latter independently of the CDA programme). It was also the first in the area to be built predominantly in facing brick - quite a contrast to the 'Scottish vernacular' derived architecture on the sites to the north, although white roughcast was still used on rear elevations.

Terraced housing at Cavendish Street, completed by the former Scottish Special Housing Association in 1984.

The ground floors of the multi-storey blocks accommodate a few shops and community rooms, but no natural focus for Laurieston has been provided. Community self-help over the years is exemplified by the replacement Gorbals Parish Church, a growing centre of community life; seats and children's playgrounds set up by the Community Council and the Glasgow Development Agency; and the Laurieston Youth Centre, Geoff Shaw's last legacy, where young people manage their own club and affairs. Still commemorated in the name of an Outdoor Group, Geoff Shaw was a charismatic Church of Scotland minister whose church was the whole of the Gorbals. He shared his life with local people, especially the young; he enabled people to use their talent in an environment which did not encourage self-confidence; he provided opportunities for people to combat unhappiness and drug problems; he fought the authorities on behalf of the rejected, or those who had lost hope; and he cherished and built on the qualities latent in the community of humour, kindness and generosity. Much loved and greatly respected, he entered politics and eventually became Convener of the former Strathclyde Regional Council. After he died, the congregation at his funeral service in Glasgow Cathedral included 'the Great and the Good' of the city. But it was Gorbals people that walked in seemingly endless line down the High Street, across the bridge, and home - to the Gorbals.

Gaps on the riverbank have been filled by the new Sheriff Court and the Glasgow Central Mosque and Islamic Centre and the south-eastern corner of Gorbals Cross has been rebuilt with a four-storey building (the Legal Centre) which extends southwards to include a new frontage for the Citizens' Theatre, the category 'B' listed auditorium of which still exists to the rear. The swathe of ground at Bedford Street, once intended for the proposed elevated structure of the Inner Ring Road's southern flank, is now, happily, proposed for housing development.

Alexander 'Greek' Thomson's Queen's Park Terrace at Eglinton Street, prior to demolition in 1980.

But the old grid-iron network of streets has almost completely disappeared from Laurieston. 27 buildings listed as of special architectural or historic interest have been lost, including entire tenement blocks in Abbotsford Place, Nicholson Street and Cumberland Street, the Gorbals John Knox Parish Church in Carlton Place, the Gorbals Public Baths and the frontage of the Citizens' Theatre in Gorbals Street, and notable tenements by the architect, Alexander 'Greek' Thomson. Demolition of Thomson's Queen's Park Terrace at 355-429 Eglinton Street and of the former St. Ninian's Wynd Church at Cathcart Road/Crown Street, both listed category 'A', followed as recently as 1980 and 1985, respectively. It is perhaps ironic to consider that, had the old Laurieston survived, its concentration of listed buildings would probably have led to designation of at least part as a conservation area.

Red sandstone tenements in Rosebery Street, Oatlands, 1997. Their recent demolition followed the failure of one of the first large-scale tenement refurbishment schemes in Glasgow.

Oatlands

Outline Comprehensive Development Area plans for the third major constituent part of Gorbals, Oatlands, were prepared, but never implemented. Although five street blocks of the worst tenements were demolished, the remaining red sandstone tenements, containing 715 dwellings, were refurbished by the Council in the 1970s, one of the first such schemes in the city. Unfortunately, the refurbishment did not prove to be a success, and the last substantial area of tenemental property in the Gorbals was demolished in 1998.

Looking eastwards from the top of the Norfolk Court flats towards Hutchesontown in 1984.

The Gorbals in the 1980s - Its Lowest Ebb

By the mid 1980's, much of the Gorbals had already acquired an air of neglect and dilapidation. The redevelopment of the area had tailed off, and the effects of poor building specifications and the lack of attention to detail in the design of the surrounding spaces were becoming increasingly apparent. Tracts of vacant ground with single-storey street corner pubs representing the remains of demolished tenements, together with the vacant deck-access blocks of Hutchesontown 'Area E' as a centrepiece, depressed the environment for local people and gave a dismal and lasting impression to visitors.

Much of the area's vitality had been extinguished. The population had fallen from over 85,000 in 1931 and 68,000 in 1951 to only 10,000. The number and variety of shops in the area had declined dramatically and the main local shopping centre - Cumberland Arcade/Queen Elizabeth Square - was unattractive and poorly designed. Mainly due to the falling population, the area's only non-denominational secondary school (Adelphi) was closed in 1984 after a mere twenty year life. Long before this, Hutcheson's Grammar School, the handsome buildings of which once graced Crown Street, had been relocated to Pollokshields in 1959. Also, the last Jewish building in the Gorbals, the 'Great Synagogue' in South Portland Street, was closed in 1974.

The worst housing problem related to the 759 flats and maisonettes in the Hutchesontown 'Area E' development at Crown Street. The first tenants had moved into 'Hutchie E' as it was better known, in August 1972, but, very quickly (within two years of completion), those in the seven-storey deck-access blocks experienced severe dampness problems. Condensation and water penetration were the results of poor insulation and lack of waterproofing at the joints in the panels which made up the structure. The building system used to create the buildings (reputedly of North African origin) had, in fact, been totally unsuited to the Scottish climate. Wallcoverings, carpets, clothing and furniture were badly damaged by fungi and many residents suffered physical illness caused by the damp atmosphere, not to mention mental health problems. In September 1980, after a concerted tenants' campaign including a long-running rent strike, the City of Glasgow District Council agreed to rehouse all of the remaining tenants. After consideration of alternative options such as refurbishment for sale, the Council agreed, in October 1984, to demolish all 759 flats and maisonettes, although the work was not actually carried out until November 1987. Proposals for large-scale shopping development on the site came to nothing.

The showpiece of twenty years previously was now in dire need of regeneration. But several years were to elapse before the Council was in a position to address tenants' concerns about lack of property maintenance and a general frustration about the lack of an overall strategy to reverse the area's decline.

Crown Street in June 1987. Demolition of the seven-storey deck-access blocks in Hutchesontown 'Area E'.

Left:-Looking eastwards over the site of the demolished Hutchesontown 'Area E' towards Queen Elizabeth Square, Cumberland Arcade (with flats above) and St. Francis' Church. This picture dates from 1991, four years after the high-rise block had received its pitched metal roof.

Below:-Queen Elizabeth Square after demolition on 12th September 1993. Tragically, a local resident was killed as the buildings were 'blown down'.

Further controversy arose in 1990 when the District Council decided to demolish the high-rise blocks at Queen Elizabeth Square. Despite ad hoc remedies to address very expensive immediate maintenance and management problems, such as a new roof, new lifts, new security measures and new community facilities, such measures had had little success in improving the blocks' popularity with tenants. After consideration of necessary further refurbishment costs amounting to £12,600,000 or £31,550 per house, and still not providing entirely satisfactory housing, the Council considered that further investment would be uneconomic and wasteful of resources. The Council's decision to demolish was, however, criticised by those (mainly modernist architects!) who considered Sir Basil Spence's blocks to be a masterpiece of modern architecture, worthy of listing as of architectural/historic interest. But, in view of the blocks' intractable problems, they were 'blown down' in 1993.

Differing opinions on the subject of Queen Elizabeth Square

"Unlike the standardised 'package deal' blocks, Spence envisioned a great monument, an idea made of concrete."

Paul Stirton

"They are the most complex of all the city's multi-storey blocks, powerful in silhouette, elevation and detail, but brutal as an environment..."

Buildings of Scotland - Glasgow

"At the time of their building ... these vertical streets were hailed as the solution to inner city problems. Now many are not so sure."

Gorbals Heritage Trails (First Edition)

"They are undoubtedly visionary and typically utopian in spirit."

Brian Edwards

"The whole scheme was looked on as a massive architectural and social experiment ... The external appearance of these giant blocks has brought much criticism, and their style has not been repeated. The dark, narrow passages are distinctly unpleasant and already, after about ten years, the staircases are similar in appearance to those in the so-called 'slums' they replaced, and far worse in smell."

Frank Worsdall

"But there are also the horrors ... Basil Spence's Gorbals and all its progeny - the ghastliness lies about us to this day as far as the eye can see."

Richard Jacques

"The powerful rhythm of their row of linked towers demonstrates Spence's clear grasp of the architectural potential of tall buildings. The play of form afforded at ground level by their piloti is truly dramatic, their design owing as much to the Japanese metabolists as to Le Corbusier."

James Dunnett

"Is he kidding us? The best thing that can happen to them is to pull them down ... they're a disaster".

Unnamed Gorbals resident, quoted in *The Scotsman*

The 1990s Regeneration of The Gorbals

Right:-Drawing of the Crown Street development, clearly showing the return to traditional streets and clearly defined open spaces (CSRP/ Hypostyle Architects).

An evolving statutory Local Plan for Gorbals (eventually adopted in 1994 after a lengthy process of consultation and refinement) laid the foundations for new development on a more human scale. The establishment of a Council-led corporate working group in 1986, followed by the Crown Street Regeneration Project and the community-based New Gorbals Housing Association gave much needed impetus towards large scale physical development. Now that the deck-access flats of Hutchesontown 'Area E', the threat of motorway construction through the middle of the Gorbals and the Queen Elizabeth Square high-rise blocks are "nothing more than a fading memory", and now that the design mistakes of the 1960s are recognised, the emphasis is presently on recreating more traditional streets and more clearly defined open spaces.

Within this context, it is interesting to note the continuing evolution of architectural approach. Discredited 1960s styles have been followed by the relative conservatism apparent in the earlier Crown Street developments. But now the architectural profession has a new-found confidence which is exhibited by some of the 'exciting' and innovative buildings being erected to herald the millennium. The commitment to high quality, the availability of better building materials and better maintenance regimes, and greater attention to detail should ensure that today's architectural innovation stands the test of time better than that of the 1960s.

Left:-New tenements under construction at Old Rutherglen Road, October 1994, with the 'Twomax' Building in the background.

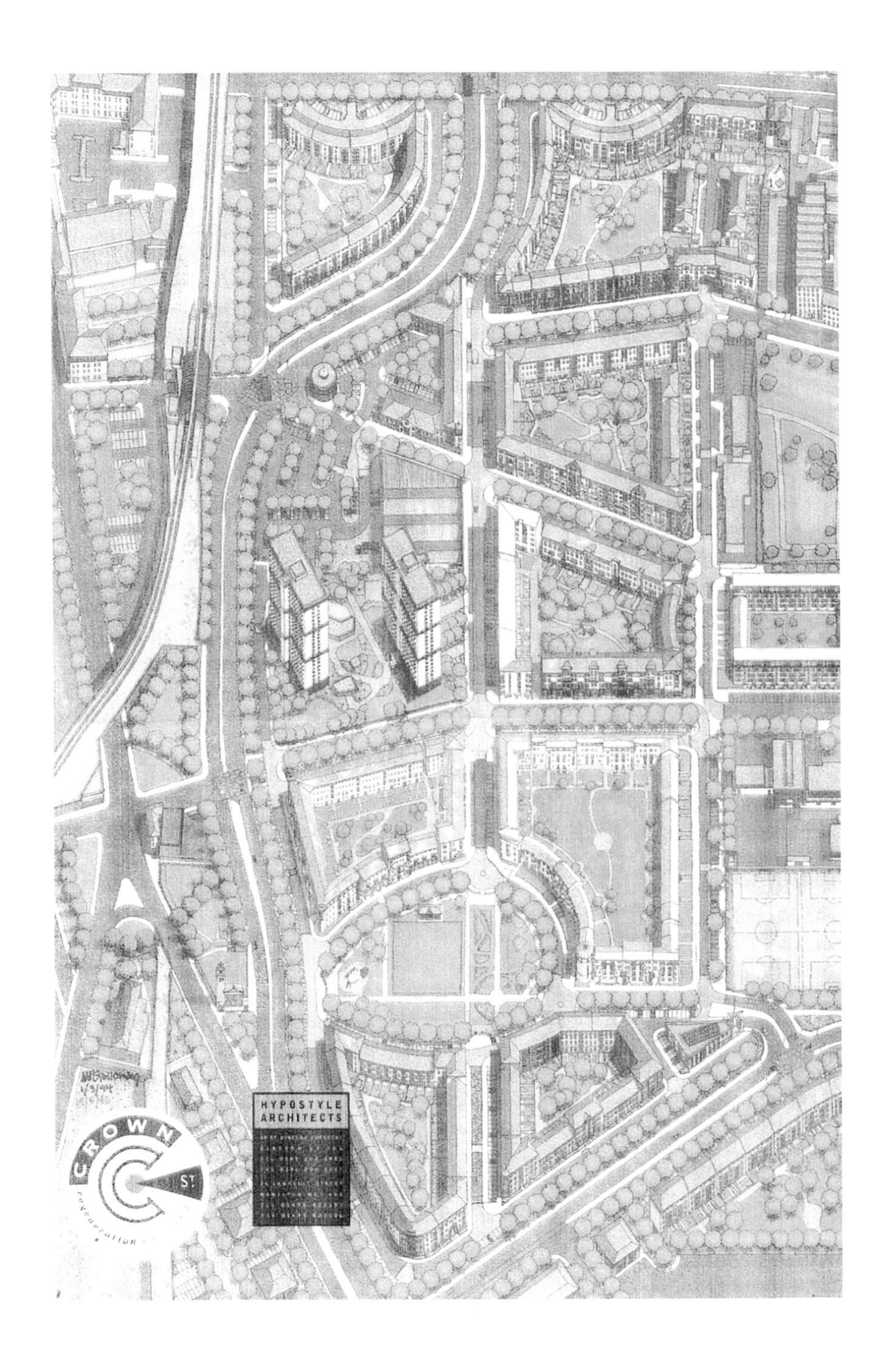
HYPOSTYLE
ARCHITECTS
CROWN
ST
regeneration

Pine Place from the pend of Benny Lynch Court - part of the Crown Street development.

Sites for nearly 3,000 new houses have been identified, and two major projects are now under way. About 1,000 of these dwellings are being provided under the auspices of the Crown Street Regeneration Project which was first promoted in 1989 by the Glasgow Development Agency. In May 1990, the winning design, by CZWG architects of London, was selected for the layout of the area. The main features of the development were to be the reintroduction of four-storey tenemental housing, a new shopping street, east-west streets with central parking and boulevard trees, and large communal back garden areas on similar lines to those at Maida Vale, London. Co-incidentally, many features of this approach have more in common with Glasgow's West End than the old Gorbals - and why not? By 1999, 598 houses were complete or under construction, 441 for owner-occupation and 157 by the New Gorbals Housing Association. Also at Crown Street, a new shopping area is being created to replace the ugly, decayed and unpopular Cumberland Arcade.

The second major housing project under way at the time of writing is at McNeil Street. Here, in 1992, the Hanover Housing Association pioneered the current regeneration of the Gorbals by building a two-storey courtyard development of sheltered housing. Since then, the New Gorbals Housing Association has concentrated its efforts in this area, having, by 1999, completed or started 188 dwellings and two augmented care facilities for the elderly.

The Gorbals' severe unemployment problems are being tackled by the Gorbals Initiative, a local enterprise company which aims to provide access for local people to the many job opportunities nearby and to stimulate local economic activity. It is based in the former Adelphi Secondary School, refurbished to a high standard in 1997 as a Training and Employment Centre.

In front of the Adelphi Centre, the City Council is building a superb new leisure centre for the Gorbals, including swimming pools and sports halls, while the category 'A' listed former St Francis' Church in Cumberland Street has been transformed into a community/learning/arts centre of the highest quality. Thus a balance is being struck between housing and other necessary developments, but much still has to be done, as will be apparent to those following the Heritage Walk. Major challenges for the future include the refurbishment of 'Greek' Thomson's Caledonia Road Church, the regeneration of Oatlands, and the completion of the riverside walkway.

Social cohesion has been largely lost through wholesale clearance, redevelopment and the more recent demolitions of 'Hutchie E', of Queen Elizabeth Square and at Oatlands. The current regeneration efforts, including attention to health, employment and education issues, set the scene for a revival of community spirit, aided by a multiplicity of voluntary local groups. It is clear that the evolution of the Gorbals' community will continue long after the large scale physical works have been completed.

The 'Gorbals East' redevelopment in the north-eastern corner of Hutchesontown, with part of the new riverside walkway on the left and the 1960s multi-storey blocks of Hutchesontown 'Area D' in the background.

THE WALK

Suggested start and finish: The Suspension bridge linking Clyde Street to Carlton Place. Approximate duration of walk:

Main Route: At least 2 hours

Main Route including Offshoots: Approximately 3 hours.

Please bear in mind that, as the regeneration of the Gorbals continues, there are bound to be changes in the details given.

Carlton Suspension Bridge - start and finish of the Heritage Walk.

1. Carlton Suspension Bridge

Cross the Clyde into Laurieston by the Carlton Suspension Bridge, erected in its current form in 1871. One of Glasgow's most beautiful bridges, it was designed by Alexander Kirkland, architect and George Martin, engineer. After dark, the bridge is floodlit, in common with many of the other Clyde bridges.

2. Carlton Place

The bridge leads to the end of South Portland Street. To the right and left stretch the classical terraces of Carlton Place, designed initially by Peter Nicholson (unhappily the only surviving piece of his work) and finished by John Baird I. The terrace on the left is the older and finer, and was built in 1802-4; the second stretch followed in 1818. Unfortunately, both terraces have lost their original western 'pavilions' or endpieces.

Since 1989, an award-winning comprehensive refurbishment of the terraces has been carried out at a total cost of over £5,000,000, the architects for the work being Philip

Carlton Place looking west, with Laurieston House immediately on the left.

Carlton Place from the suspension bridge.

Cocker & Partners. The exteriors of the buildings have been restored to their original symmetry and appearance, the roadway has been reinstated with granite setts, the pavements have been laid with Caithness Stone slabs and suitable new railings and lampposts have been provided. Both the tall lampposts on the river side of the street and the small standards set in pairs in front of the central pavilions are reproductions of 19th century Glasgow examples.

Numbers 71-73 Carlton Place (in the right-hand block) have been remodelled as the Prince and Princess of Wales Hospice which offers inpatient and outpatient services for those suffering from terminal illnesses, and support for their relatives.

3. Laurieston House

The central pavilion of the left-hand block (Laurieston House) was the home of James Laurie who not only commissioned this terrace but bought and developed much of the land behind it, to create the district which now bears his name, Laurieston. James Laurie had great dreams for the land he bought, and exacted high standards from the architects he employed. He visualised a suburb of classical dignity for the business and professional men who wanted to escape from the crowded central city. The heart of this area was to be a great academy providing education for all (men) - the sons of the middle classes during the day, craftsmen and apprentices at night. There were to be covered markets, churches and plenty of gardens and open spaces, all set along wide, spacious streets. Carlton Place represents the only significant part of this dream to have survived.

Laurieston House is considered to have the most handsome interior of its date in Glasgow, including an impressive staircase and exceptional plaster work, reputedly by Italian artists brought to this country by George IV to decorate Windsor Castle The building is at present closed to the public, but has been made wind and watertight by the Strathclyde Building Preservation Trust with a view to eventual purchase and restoration by an occupier willing to allow a degree of public access.

4. South Portland Street

Leaving Carlton Place, go southwards along South Portland Street. Just before its junction with Oxford Street, in the centre of the road, are preserved two strips of neatly-laid setts as a reminder of the one-time tram route to Carlton Place from the south.

The next section of the street, while preserving none of the original buildings, encapsulates much of the evolution of the caring society since the mid 19th century. The first building on the left, a rather unlovely composition of concrete and dark brown brick, was built as replacement premises for the Guild of Aid, a charity established in Victorian times to benefit the 'deserving poor', saving lives and enhancing living for many. They were the pioneers of playschools, drama and dancing classes, roof-top gardens, holidays for needy families and, almost certainly, the first Glasgow experiment in sheltered housing for old people. Now the building accommodates the offices of Alzheimer Scotland Action on Dementia.

The adjoining premises on South Portland Street still belong to the Glasgow Medical Missionary Society which established a Dispensary in Oxford Street in 1867. There the poor could get free medical treatment and medicine, medical students were educated about the problems of the poor and religious services were held on Sundays. The old dispensary building disappeared in 1974, but the evangelical traditions continue. Next door is the Salvation Army Centre, and beyond that is the taller red sandstone building which formerly housed Gorbals' second free library (closed in 1986) but is now the Glasgow Centre for the Deaf which includes the John Ross Memorial Church for the Deaf.

Prior to the 1960s redevelopment of the area, the vista ahead continued to the Georgian tenements of Abbotsford Place, diminishing into the distance. Now the view is abruptly closed by the single-storey, flat-roofed St. John's RC Primary School (and Laurieston Day Nursery).

Looking to the left (east) along Oxford Street, the older building on the right is the Strathclyde Police Training Centre, the functions of which are due to relocate in the year 2000. This is a well-proportioned building, completed in 1895 as a police office and barracks and designed by A B McDonald, City Engineer. Closing the view here is the Sheriff Courthouse (item 39).

Former stables and warehouse, 21-25 Carlton Court.

5. 21-25 Carlton Court - Former Stables and Warehouse

Retrace your steps a short distance and turn left into Carlton Court, which leads to Bridge Street. On the right, about half way along, are the former stables and warehouse of the Clyde Shipping Company. Dating from the period 1880-85, this building consisted of a three-storey warehouse and smithy at the front and stables, hay loft and machine shop to the rear. It is the last example of its kind in Glasgow and was converted into offices in 1987, successfully retaining the old stable yard and the main features of the warehouse block. Note the central dormer-head and goods hoist over the former door openings on the first, second and attic floors.

6. Cumbrae House

Beyond the stables and leading to the corner with Bridge Street is the Art Deco Cumbrae House, clad with glazed tiles and featuring metal panels between the first and second floor windows. Originally designed by Launcelot H. Ross, it was built in 1937-8 as showrooms and offices for Cowen's Ideal Trading Stamp Company (Glasgow) Ltd and restored as modern office space in 1988 by the Houston Bryce Partnership. Directly across Bridge Street from the end of Carlton Court was the original site of the Bridge Street Station (see item 8).

Opposite:-Cumbrae House: south elevation facing Carlton Court.

7. 20-22 Bridge Street - Former Commercial Bank

Turn left into Bridge Street. The isolated building on the corner opposite was built for the Commercial Bank of Scotland, with flats above. It is dated 1884 and was designed in Early Renaissance style, most likely by the firm of Bruce and Hay, although detail on the facade suggests that Hugh Barclay of H. & D. Barclay may have been the architect. Remarkably, the ground floor exterior has survived intact.

Former Commercial Bank, 20-22 Bridge Street.

HOUSE

8. Bridge Street Station

Further south along Bridge Street, the long four-storey and attic building on the opposite side represents an interesting piece of industrial archaeology. Behind the shop fascia in the centre was the booking hall of the old Bridge Street Station which, in its original form, predated the Central as the principal passenger terminus of the city. Above the flanking stair entrances are terracotta plaques, the left dated 'AD 1890', and the other displaying the Caledonian Railway's lion rampant. The station building, converted into flats in 1993, was designed by the architect James Miller and the engineer George Graham. The former Station Hotel, the old four-storey building which adjoins to the right, was also recently converted into flats. The Caledonian Railway's Bridge Street Station replaced the terminal station of the Glasgow, Paisley and Greenock Railway, a white sandstone building of 1841 with a "handsome portico and stately columns", once situated further north opposite the end of Carlton Court.

9. 63-67 Bridge Street - Former Savings Bank

A little further along the left side of the street is the former south branch of the Savings Bank of Glasgow, now a Greek restaurant. The bank was inserted into an existing mid 19th century building in 1888 by the architect, John Gordon. On the ground floor are six paired granite Ionic columns (a further two are missing) and a fine wrought iron gate. The

Left:-Bridge Street looking south from Carlton Place, c.1870. The columned frontage of the original Bridge Street Station, built in 1841, can be seen on the right (Mitchell Library).

Right:-The replacement Bridge Street Station building, long since closed and recently converted into flats.

interior contains an impressive domed banking hall with balustrade, an elaborate plaster cornice and fine woodwork.

10. 144-150 Norfolk Street/69-71 Bridge Street

Further on again, the corner tenement on the left was designed by James Miller, built in 1898 and contains many interesting architectural details such as the octagonal turret rising from first to third floors at the corner. It features 'Glasgow Style' architectural elements in its oriel windows, bold chimney stacks and a saucer dome, with richly carved Edwardian Baroque detail. The attractive spiral staircase at 148 Norfolk Street starts, unconventionally, at first floor level. *In front, to the south and east, stretch the wide open spaces of Laurieston. A lot of the past has been swept away - the broad streets lined by classical tenements, the dance halls, churches, shops, the Great Synagogue, the teeming masses of people. It is a truism that if Laurieston's reconstruction had come a few years later, we might have had a good measure of rehabilitation rather than wholesale destruction. But at the time, new houses seemed to be the only answer to the decay and distress that absentee landlords, overcrowding and disrepair had caused.*

Left:-Terracotta plaques above the stair entrances to the former Bridge Street Station.

Detail of the turret at the corner of Bridge Street and Norfolk Street.

11. The Coliseum

As you continue up Eglinton Street past the reconstructed Bridge Street Underground Station and its surrounding car park, the vast bulk of the Coliseum comes into view beyond the trees. It is a large Flemish-style music hall, opened in 1905, and designed by the renowned theatre architect, Frank Matcham. The building is distinguished by its octagonal red sandstone tower, topped by a domed cupola which formerly enclosed a revolving 'Coliseum' sign. Its capacity was 2,700 persons. At first, it was the home of variety, pantos and, in 1920, Wagner's 'Ring'. Converted to a cinema in 1925, the first 'talkie' in Glasgow, The Jazz Singer starring Al Jolson, was shown here in 1929. In 1962, after an unbroken run as the main ABC cinema for the south side of the city, it was

The Coliseum, Eglinton Street.

converted to 'Cinerama' with the largest screen in Britain, but the original interior was destroyed and the exterior was disfigured by a new sheet metal facade. The cinema was closed in 1980; but after a short period in Council ownership, having been bought to make way for a motorway (the south flank of the city's Inner Ring Road) which never came to fruition, it was converted into a bingo hall.

12. The 'New' Bedford

Further on, on the opposite side of Bedford Street, is the 'New' Bedford, a 1932 cinema by Lennox and McMath in Art Deco style, run for many years (1936-1973) by Green's, subsequently a further bingo hall and now closed. It was erected in only nine months to replace the fire-damaged, original Bedford Cinema which had been converted from a former United Free Church. Until repainting in 1988, the facade featured a night-sky mosaic and coloured zig-zags round the central arch.

Beyond the four-storey, white harled Council flats on the left (Eglinton Court, designed and built by Crudens Ltd.), stands Gorbals Parish Church. It is a low, modern building, opened in 1975. Unfortunately, the quality of its architecture does not begin to match that of its predecessor on much the same site, the Laurieston Renwick Church of 1869. However, the congregation hopes to move once again to a more central site at Crown Street in the near future.

13. Railway Arches

Along the south side of Cumberland Street is a line of railway arches, converted into industrial units in 1987. The construction of this elevated railway over the period 1864-67 followed extensive demolition of property, much of it relatively new at the time. This development by the City of Glasgow Union Railway, combined with the earlier development of railway termini at Gushetfaulds, slowed down the southward expansion of Laurieston, and was one of the reasons for Laurie's plans never being completely realised. In 1900, the original line of arches was widened to form a high level, four platform station (Eglinton Street Station, later renamed Cumberland Street Station) by the Glasgow and South Western Railway. The station was closed in the 1960s. The red sandstone entrance block still survives, although in poor condition, but the 1900 additions were demolished in 1987.

14. Birthplace of Sir Hugh Roberton

Continue under the railway bridge. On the left, above the 'Wellcroft Place' nameplate on the four-storey flats, can be seen a plaque to commemorate the birthplace of Sir Hugh Roberton (1874-1952), founder and conductor of the Glasgow Orpheus Choir.

*On the opposite side of Eglinton Street at this point was Port Eglinton, built in 1811, the terminal basin of the Glasgow, Paisley and Johnstone Canal. This canal was intended to run as far as Ardrossan, but was never completed. Users of the canal included William Dixon, local colliery proprietor, and founder of the Govan Iron Works (**see item C on page 74**). The canal was not long in existence for, in 1881, the Glasgow and South Western Railway, as owner, obtained powers to fill the waterway and construct a railway along its length.*

15. Former Eglinton Congregational Church

Further up Eglinton Street, adjacent to the red brick housing completed by the Scottish Special Housing Association in 1984, is the former Eglinton Congregational Church, dated 1866 and designed by John Burnet Senior in the Gothic style. Note the pointed arches and angel heads above the doors and the original Gothic detailed cast-iron railings. The building is currently empty, its remarkable interior decoration of 1895 having been destroyed through dry rot and water penetration.

Before railway construction, a cavalry barracks, built in 1821, and later converted to the Poorhouse for Govan Parish, was situated on the opposite side of Eglinton Street from here. As a barracks, the building was a base for the suppression of the working-class riots which accompanied the Industrial Revolution; as a Poorhouse, it catered for the unfortunates of Gorbals Parish, as well as the growing areas of Laurieston and Hutchesontown which remained in Govan Parish.

Angel heads above the doors of the former Congregational Church, Eglinton Street.

16. Former Abbotsford Primary School

Turn the corner into Devon Street and straight in front you will see the former Abbotsford School. This is the oldest surviving school building in Gorbals but was closed in 1996 and is due to be converted into flats. With Sir Hugh Roberton as a former pupil, it is perhaps no coincidence that the school had a long tradition of choirs. Designed by H. & D. Barclay and dating from 1879; it was the first school in Glasgow to be built to a pattern with which many Glaswegians are familiar - the open central hall with classes round it and an upper floor of rooms opening from a balcony. The carved heads above the doors, both front and back, are of eminent Scots. On the Devon Street frontage, the heads represent John Knox and David Livingstone. The Italianate style of the main building is reflected in the design of the adjacent two-storey janitor's house.

The former Abbotsford Primary School, as viewed from the west.

St. Andrew's Works from Eglinton Toll in 1917, showing the building in its original form as a coal-fired power station (City Archives).

17. St. Andrew's Works

Before turning left into Pollokshaws Road, it is possible to see the large, red brick St. Andrew's Works up the road to the right. It was built in 1899-1900 as an electricity generating station by Glasgow Corporation (architect - Andrew Myles), and partly converted in 1937 to a printing works.

18. Former Chalmers Free Church

A little down Pollokshaws Road is the former Chalmers Free Church which, in common with the other buildings in the block, was designed by H. & D. Barclay in a vaguely Italianate style. The front has an impressive semi-circular portico with two Ionic columns, above which is a wheel window. The congregation moved here from a church designed by

The former Chalmers Free Church, Pollokshaws Road, now converted into residential accommodation.

Caledonia Road Church in 1965, prior to the demolition of adjoining tenements, also designed by Alexander Thomson (Jim Mackintosh Photography).

Alexander 'Greek' Thomson in Govan Street (now called Ballater Street) which had been partially demolished to make way for the Glasgow Union Railway. In 1994, the building was successfully converted into supported housing accommodation for 40 single people, the project being named after James Shields, the former Lord Provost of Glasgow, who died in 1995.

19. Caledonia Road Church

At the foot of Pollokshaws Road, turn sharp right opposite the public house built into the railway arches. A short distance up Cathcart Road stand the remains of Alexander 'Greek' Thomson's Caledonia Road Church, a category 'A' listed building considered to be of national or international importance.

Built in 1856-57 in Thomson's Greek style, it has a number of noteworthy architectural features such as its masterly square tower, the Ionic portico at first floor level, the masonry

Caledonia Road Church in 1998.

laid in alternating broad and narrow bands, and the unusual base course of irregularly shaped stones. The interior was bright and colourful, in contrast to most Victorian churches. This outstanding building ceased to be used for worship in 1962 and was gutted by fire in 1965. Stabilisation of the shell was completed in 1969 and, following years of indifference, only now is a serious attempt being made by the local authority to achieve restoration. In conjunction with other development agencies and landowners, the City Council is attempting, through the preparation of a Development/ Design Guide, to unlock the development potential of the area and provide the church shell with an appropriate built context and beneficial future use.

To the north and east of the Caledonia Road Church is Hutchesontown, planned and developed by the Hutcheson's Hospital Trust in the early 19th century as a new town which would accommodate cotton mills and ancillary industries such as machine manufacturers, dyeworks and builders yards. The Trust laid out the town on a grid pattern, with broad streets and houses not so grand as those in Laurieston, but at first, at least, of a reasonable standard. In its midst, at Crown Street, they put their great school, popularly known as 'Hutchies'. But the grid system produced hollow squares of houses many of which all too soon were filled with back tenements, small workshops, even little factories. House sizes were reduced; the fresh air became polluted; sanitary arrangements were insufficient. Finally the new town deteriorated too drastically to meet healthy standards of living. So, rather earlier than in Laurieston, the bulldozers moved in, whole streets disappeared, and redevelopment took place.

Hutcheson's Grammar School, once a feature of Crown Street, Hutchesontown.

20. Crown Street Regeneration Project

Cross the busy Laurieston Road towards the right hand side of the new tenements opposite and continue into Alexander Crescent (named after Alexander Row, a row of houses once situated close to the Govan Iron Works nearby). Here, on the site of the notorious damp-infested flats and maisonettes of Hutchesontown 'Area E' (occupied by tenants, 1972-1980), the Crown Street Regeneration Project is bringing back a traditional street network, lined mainly by four-storey tenements. This development, which aims to provide about 1,000 houses and a new shopping 'street' for the Gorbals, sets a new standard for the area's regeneration in terms of urban design, architecture and building materials. The housing on the left, facing the 'Greek' Thomson Church and the new Gorbals Park on the right, was built by Stewart Milne Homes to the designs of the Holmes Partnership. Its most distinctive features are the stone-clad corner towers, the southern of which has a close visual relationship with the former church. Beyond the junction with Crown Street, the curved block of three-storey townhouses and strong rotunda feature at the corner of Naburn Gate are part of another development of private housing, this time by Miller Partnerships, their architects being Cooper Cromar.

Turn left into Crown Street. On the right hand side are two notable developments by the community-based New

Flats and townhouses nearing completion in Alexander Crescent, with the Caledonia Road Church in the background.

Above:-Elder and Cannon's design for the housing on the east side of Crown Street, between Alexander Crescent and Cumberland Street, the clients being the community-based New Gorbals Housing Association.

Right:-Cumberland Street, Gorbals, showing new tenements by Tay Homes and, in the background, the Sandiefield Road flats, the only remaining parts of the ill-fated Hutchesontown 'Area E' development.

Gorbals Housing Association which is providing 25% of the dwellings in the Crown Street development, firstly by Elder & Cannon, and secondly, opposite the 24-storey flats which remain from the Hutchesontown 'Area E' development, by Page & Park. Both schemes, with their distinctive monopitch roofs, are more architecturally 'adventurous' than previous developments on the Crown Street site and go some way towards providing the sense of scale required at this central location.

Before turning right into Errol Gardens, note the supermarket on the left and the two further tenemental private housing developments on the right. The supermarket with its ancillary shop units was designed by Young & Gault architects to a relatively high standard of exterior finish and design, including the use of natural sandstone. Although the lack of building height at such a prominent location is to be regretted, the standards of construction are much superior to those normally expected of commercial developments outwith established town centres or conservation areas. On the north frontage, the building features sculptural work by Jack Sloan - his images of the contents of supermarket baskets overflowing from the tops of classical columns. These are only one example of the many artworks which adorn the Crown Street development - all developments here have been required to include artworks to the value of one per cent of construction costs.

The two blocks of four-storey tenements further up the right hand (east) side of Crown Street were the private housing element of the first phase of the Regeneration Project, completed in 1995. The more distant block with the corner tower was Miller Partnerships' first development in the

Drawing of the tower at the corner of Crown Street/St. Ninian Terrace and Old Rutherglen Road, designed by the Holmes Partnership for Millers, the private housing developers.

Pine Place and Benny Lynch Court, housing designed for the New Gorbals Housing Association by Cooper Cromar, architects.

Gorbals, designed by the Holmes Partnership. Wimpey Homes (architects - Cooper Cromar) built the nearer block, with shops all along the Crown Street frontage.

Turn right into Errol Gardens; where this street meets Pine Place, look left to see more of the New Gorbals Housing Association's exemplary housing stock, which, like the neighbouring Wimpey development, was designed by Cooper Cromar. Opposite the Health Centre is a row of attractive terraced housing, while closing the view at the end of the street is a four-storey tenement pierced by a pend leading into Benny Lynch Court, another group of low-rise dwellings.

Turn right into Pine Place. The handsome townhouses on the right form part of Hypostyle Architects' design for Tay Homes.

21. Blackfriars Primary School

Turn left into Cumberland Street, following the north boundary of Blackfriars Primary School. The 1960s development replaced the street at this point with a hard surfaced 'pedestrian area' subdivided with a meaningless pattern of low brick walls. The current regeneration process is restoring the traditional street character, whilst discouraging unnecessary through traffic. This school (in common with St. Francis' Primary at Old Rutherglen Road)

Hutcheson Square in 1955, once notable for its swing park and bandstand. One of the trees in the picture still remains within the grounds of Blackfriars Primary School.

was an integral part of the original redevelopment scheme, built in 1961-64 and designed by J. L. Gleave and Partners. It is interesting to compare the quality of this building with the later single-storey St John's Primary School in Laurieston which provides such an unsatisfactory visual closure to the end of South Portland Street (item 4). In the school grounds are a wildlife garden and 'rainforest play area', the provision of which was co-ordinated by the Glasgow Junior Chamber of Commerce and the Gorbals Initiative. In the playground on the opposite side of the school buildings is a sparce reminder of the old Gorbals which can be viewed from Camden Terrace. A solitary tree, guarded by metal railings, remains from Hutcheson Square, once the scene of a well-used children's playground and the venue for Salvation Army band concerts on Sundays.

22. Hutchesontown 'Area D' - Scottish Special Housing Association

Further along on the right, the four-storey maisonette blocks form part of the 'Area D' development, originally built by the Scottish Special Housing Association (SSHA) and now owned and managed by Scottish Homes. One of the more successful aspects of 1960s Gorbals, these houses and their surroundings have been considerably upgraded over the past decade. In the background, the four 24-storey blocks are in process of renewal, having already been provided with sophisticated closed-circuit television and district heating systems. At the same time, the complicated layout of concrete decks and underpasses once thought suitable for the base of the blocks has been replaced with pleasant greenery and high-quality paving (this can be viewed by walkers following Offshoot No. 1).

23. St Francis' Centre and Former Friary

On the opposite side of Cumberland Street, further new streets of housing are due to replace the unsightly and rundown shopping and community facilities which were once the centrepiece of the Hutchesontown/Part Gorbals redevelopment. It is perhaps ironic that the next building on the left, a rare 19th century survival in this part of the Gorbals, should outlive the 1960s failures and become a focus for community life at the start of the 21st century. This, the former St. Francis' RC Church, with a statue of St. Francis at the top of the stair turret at the near corner, has a fascinating history.

The first Franciscan friary and church in Glasgow was dedicated in 1477, on a site almost opposite the offices of the *Glasgow Herald* and the *Evening Times* in Albion Street in the City Centre. There was a long gap between its suppression at the time of the Reformation and the reappearance of the Friars in 1868. True to the tradition of serving where poverty attacked most keenly, they bought land in Hutchesontown, and the first church, a small brick temporary structure, was opened in 1868. The friary, designed by Gilbert Blount, was started in 1870 and the foundations of the present church building were laid in 1880. This replacement building, by the architects Pugin & Pugin, in Early Decorated style, was magnificent, visually and acoustically, but it was vacated by the Franciscan Order in 1994.

The former St. Francis' Church and Friary, now successfully converted into the Gorbals' main community, learning and arts centre and flats for the elderly.

Opposite:-Interior of the St. Francis' Centre, converted by the City Council from the former St. Francis' Church (David Mitchell).

Rather than let the building suffer through deterioration and neglect, a partnership headed by the Glasgow Building Preservation Trust has successfully met the challenge of finding a new use. The former church has been ingeniously converted by the City Council into the Gorbals' main community, learning and arts centre. The architects - Page & Park - have successfully and impressively created three storeys of meeting space in an oak-panelled building comfortably located within the original structure, while plenty space remains for concerts and theatrical productions. The friars' old private chapel at first floor level has been retained, as have a number of elaborate stone altars, now protected by screens. Visitors are welcome to enter the St Francis' Centre to appreciate the fine interior and the quality of the recent alterations, completed in 1997 and officially opened by Sir Jimmy Savile and Bailie James Mutter in August 1998.

The adjoining friary building was converted at the same time, and by the same architects, into amenity flats for the elderly, now the property of the New Gorbals Housing Association. Finance was provided by Scottish Homes, Historic Scotland and by the National Trust for Scotland as part of its rolling programme of works to ensure the future use of historic buildings. The quality of the conversion work on the former church and friary buildings has been recognised by awards from the Glasgow Institute of Architects in 1997 and the Civic Trust in 1998. A history and guide book, by Tony Devlin, and published to mark the renewal of the buildings, is available.

After passing the front of the former friary, the main route of the heritage walk proceeds to the left, down Sandyfaulds Street. Items of considerable interest can, however, be found through a diversion, straight ahead, to the Southern Necropolis and then to McNeil Street.

FIRST OFFSHOOT FROM MAIN ROUTE

A. Gatehouse to the Southern Necropolis

Follow Cumberland Street to its junction with Caledonia Road, passing the Scottish Homes' multi-storey blocks on your left. Across the road is the Southern Necropolis, first laid out in 1840 to provide a dignified and beautiful burial ground for a greatly increased population. The entrance gateway tower dates from 1848 and was designed by Charles Wilson. Access to its interior is no longer encouraged, but, in recent years, an early visitors book containing the signatures of impressed visitors from all over the United Kingdom and Europe was recovered from the building by local children. Cemeteries were big news in the early nineteenth century when the problems in providing adequate burial space to cater for the results of urban growth were becoming apparent. Note the Norman influence in the mouldings round the first floor windows before passing through the archway into the central section of the cemetery.

Layout plan of the Southern Necropolis derived from the 25 inch Ordnance Survey map of 1865. The details superimposed, and the information tabulated below, are based on the work of Colin Mackie.

B. The Southern Necropolis

The cemetery, which contains more than a quarter of a million burials, replaced the original Gorbals Burial Ground at Old Rutherglen Road (item 24) which had become severely overcrowded, and held two of the dreaded mass-burial pits which had resulted from smallpox epidemics. The Southern

Gatehouse of the Southern Necropolis.

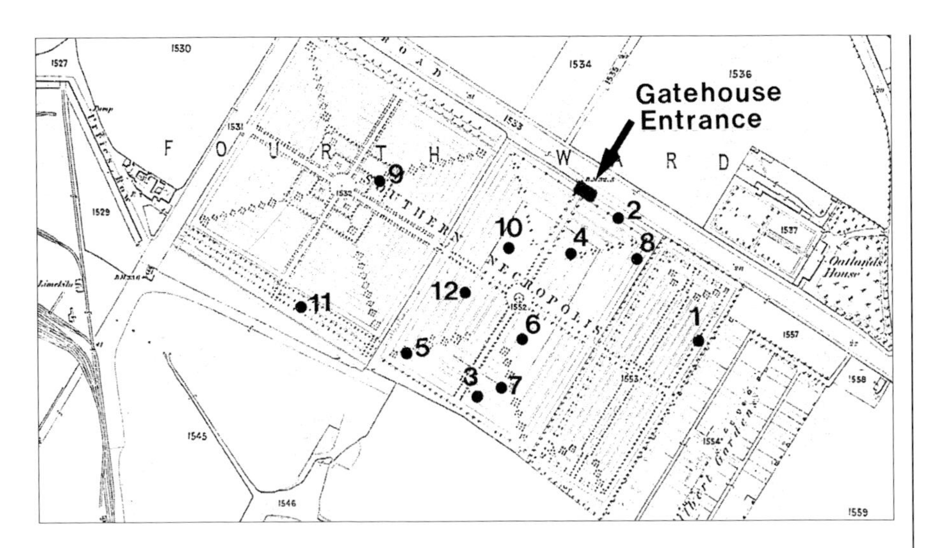

SOUTHERN NECROPOLIS - KEY TO HEADSTONES/BURIALS

No.	Burial	Life Dates	Significance/Achievements
1.	Sir Thomas Lipton	1850-1931	Famous for his chain of grocers shops and for his sailing exploits. In the same lair are buried his parents who ran a shop in Crown Street.
2.	Dr. Nathaniel Paterson	1787-1871	Grandson of Robert Paterson, the original of Sir Walter Scott's Old Mortality.
3.	John Robertson	1782-1868	Designed and built the engine of the Comet, Europe's first sea-going steamship.
4.	James Seath	1820-1903	Designed and built the first Cluthas, small steamships first used as ferries but latterly mainly associated with pleasure trips 'doon the watter'.
5.	The Geddes family		Officers of the Glasgow Humane Society which has saved many from drowning in the Clyde (stone lying flat on ground).
6.	Captain James Smart	1804-1870	Became Chief Constable of Glasgow after involvement with the Bread Riots.
7.	Hugh MacDonald	1817-1860	Prolific writer on social issues; pioneer of ramblers' clubs; famous for his book, *Rambles Round Glasgow* (small stone lying on ground).
8.	Peter Ferguson	1801-1885	Temperance leader; founder of the Band of Hope in Glasgow.
9.	Alexander 'Greek' Thomson	1817-1875	Architect of Caledonia Road Church and much of old Gorbals (grave currently unmarked - lair to left of 'John Brown' stone).
10.	James Goldie	1844-1913	Master craftsman who carried out William Leiper's design for Glasgow's 'Doge's Palace', the former Templeton's carpet factory overlooking Glasgow Green.
11.	Wee Willie Whyte	died,1858	Street musician, a great favourite in his time.
12.	'The Necropolis Ghost'		'The lady turns her head, just after you pass'.

Necropolis is in three sections - the Eastern Section, the Central, and, by far the largest, the Western. Some of the most interesting burials are located as shown on the plan on the previous page. In addition are the graves of Robert Paterson and sons, manufacturers of vinegar and Camp Coffee; Allan Glen who endowed the Glasgow school which bore his name; and Charles Wilson, the architect of Park Circus.

These include some of the great and the good, but the graves of the many lesser known families are amongst the most impressive. Notice the memorials to men who died overseas and the vast numbers of young children who died - in 1841, children under twelve accounted for 57% of burials. Only 4% of burials were of adults who lived beyond 60 years. By 1871, children under twelve formed 48.7% of total burials; 20% of those buried were over 60 years old. A full account of the history of the Southern Necropolis can be found in *City of the Dead*, edited by Charlotte Hutt, also published by Glasgow City Libraries and Archives.

C. Dixon's Blazes

Over the back wall of the Southern Necropolis, the industrial estate occupies the site of the former Govan Colliery and Iron Works - Dixon's Blazes - the great blast furnaces that lit up the night sky of Gorbals for generations. In 1849, it was written, in *Glasgow Past and Present*, that "the bright glare cheers the long winter night, and at the same time does the work of a score of policemen, by scaring away the rogues and vagabonds who so plentifully infest other and darker parts of the City". Govan Colliery came first, managed and then leased by William Dixon. It was he who was the second cause of the curtailment of Laurie's plans for Laurieston - for he was a railway pioneer who ran his coals across the southern part of Laurieston and then into Tradeston, down the middle of West Street to wharves on the Clyde, despite fierce legal battles including action in Parliament by Glasgow Town Council against the Pollok and Govan Railway Bill. The iron works with the five blast furnaces were developed by his son William. It is a pity that no traces were preserved of this heart of Glasgow's heavy industrial heritage, but it is worth noting that the present Dixon's Blazes Industrial Estate, created by Taylor Woodrow Industrial Estates Ltd., was the first private venture of its kind in Scotland.

The former Hutchesontown Library at McNeil Street, now converted into the Gorbals Economic Development Centre.

D. Former Hutchesontown District Library

From the Gatehouse of the Southern Necropolis, turn right along busy Caledonia Road and cross to Silverfir Street on the opposite side. At the end of Silverfir Street, turn left into Waterside Street and right across to McNeil Street. On your left is the former Hutchesontown Library, designed by the Inverness architect James Robert Rhind and now the Gorbals Economic Development Centre. The library was part of Glasgow's original public library system which consisted of the Mitchell Library and sixteen district libraries, and which was partly endowed by Andrew Carnegie. The building is distinguished by beautifully carved architectural and sculptural detail including the frieze showing St. Mungo flanked by maidens above the entrance, gryphons supporting the top of the tower and the female figure holding a book as the finial. Mounted on the south gable is a sculpture called The Three Muses, designed and executed in 1994 by the Gorbals Arts Project in conjunction with Bellarmine Arts Association and the pupils of St. Francis' Primary School. The inter-war tenements on the opposite side of the street are situated on the site of Todd and Higginbotham's Cotton Mill, one of the most famous in Glasgow. The mill was relocated here after the demolition in 1846-47 of previous premises at Kingston, removed to make way for a harbour extension.

Above:-McNeil Street, showing completed 'streetscape' works and looking south towards the Hutchesontown 'Area D' flats.

Left:-The centre of the Gorbals East Renewal Area - new housing for the New Gorbals Housing Association designed by Elder & Cannon and Page & Park.

E. Gorbals East Renewal Area - New Housing

Further along the street is a further example of area-wide renewal. First on the left is the development which pioneered the Gorbals' current regeneration efforts - a two-storey courtyard development of sheltered housing designed by Baxter, Clark and Paul for the Hanover Housing Association. All the other new housing developments between here and Ballater Street are the work of the New Gorbals Housing Association which is primarily responsible for the extensive 'streetscape' improvements in this vicinity (which include artwork panels and ornamental bollards in the form of pine cones by the Gorbals Arts Project). The rather

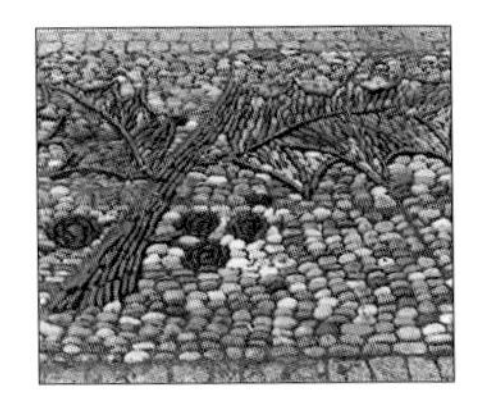

Public art as part of the McNeil Street 'streetscape' works.

Below, left:-The southern tower of the St. Andrew's Suspension Bridge with reproduction lamps provided as part of the 1997 restoration.

Below, right:-McNeil Street in 1976, looking south from St. Andrew's Suspension Bridge. The United Co-operative Bakery operated on both sides of the street, the original 1885 building being on the right.

unconventional-looking 'villa' block of flats at the near corner with Hayfield Street was designed by Elder & Cannon, architects. Facing a small urban square in Hayfield Street are contemporary and earlier housing blocks by Page & Park, together with a scheme by Simister Monaghan, the use of different architects being a deliberate attempt to introduce diversity. The housing at McNeil Gardens, leading through to the riverside and new sections of walkway, was also designed by Page & Park.

F. St. Andrew's Suspension Bridge

Continue north across Ballater Street to St. Andrew's Suspension Bridge. The whole street block on the left was occupied by the United Co-operative Bakery, built in 1885 and demolished in the 1970s. The building, designed by Bruce and Hay, looked more like a French chateau than a bakery - but it provided loaves and rolls, cakes and biscuits for a large proportion of the City's tables. Beyond the bakery site is the Strathclyde Distillery, founded in 1925, which manufactures whisky for several well-known brands and spirits for gin and vodka.

The suspension bridge, dating from 1853-5 and built largely of cast-iron, is category 'A' listed and was extensively refurbished and repainted by the City Council in 1997. Originally designed by Neil Robson (engineer) and Charles O' Neill (architect), it was built to provide access for workers between Bridgeton and Hutchesontown, and replaced a ferry. Now it gives access to Glasgow Green through which visitors

Opposite:-St. Andrew's Suspension Bridge.

can walk back to the City Centre. Alternatively, you can return to the main route of the heritage walk via McNeil Street, Hayfield Street, Moffat Street and Old Rutherglen Road. Within the Green is the People's Palace, a most interesting museum of Glasgow's history. Here, in the Winter Gardens, refreshments can be purchased as an interlude in the walk.

MAIN ROUTE (Continued)

From Cumberland Street, proceed northwards up Sandyfaulds Street and across the edge of the development site to Old Rutherglen Road where you should turn left. Here, in front of a red-and-yellow-brick block which forms part of the New Gorbals Housing Association's first development, designed by Page & Park, architects, walkers from the first offshoot rejoin the main walk and proceed westwards along Old Rutherglen Road. The vacant site on the left was the site of the Queen Elizabeth Square high-rise blocks, until their demolition in 1993 and new housing development is scheduled to restore traditional street frontages to both sides of Old Rutherglen Road at this point.

24. Gorbals Burial Ground

Further along, on the left, is another welcome green oasis in the centre of Hutchesontown. Now generally known as the 'Rose Garden', this is the old graveyard of Gorbals Parish; dating from about 1751, the original part comprised for many years a detached portion of the parish encircled by the then enormous Govan Parish. Round the walls, some interesting stones remain. On your right, entering at the gate at the far end of the Old Rutherglen Road frontage, are a few stones with no inscription, other than trade symbols. The first one is the stone of a baker with crossed 'peels' - the long shovels

Trade symbols on headstones in the old graveyard of Gorbals Parish.

used for lifting bread in and out of ovens. The second has not been identified. The third carries the picks of a collier. The fourth is the stone of a miller - the upper millstone was supported on a metal piece called a 'rind', and two crossed rinds making a pattern called a mouline are the sign of a miller.

Another interesting stone commemorates John Mackenzie of the Gaelic Chapel. The Gaelic services were held in the first Parish Church, built in 1732 (replaced by the now demolished church in Carlton Place, in 1810). At that time there was a large Highland element in the population. Notice too, Lair 479 - dedicated to James & Gavin Laurie and their heirs, and Lair 489 - the grave of John Wilson, Parish Clerk, who was also the master of the parish school and distinguished for his mathematical abilities. He was a man of many interests. Originally he had been schoolmaster in Tarbolton, Ayrshire where he dabbled, sometimes not very successfully, in medicine and instant diagnosis. He is 'Dr. Hornbook' of Burns' poem *Death and Doctor Hornbook* where Death complains of being beaten in his hunt for victims by Dr. Hornbook. Burns, however, wrote the poem after Mr. Wilson had left Tarbolton, and they appear to have stayed good friends.

At Lair 500 is another interesting stone, though in a way it is a near-miss for Gorbals. It is a stone dedicated to Walter Neilson, Engineer, of Govan Colliery, by his sons John and James. John is buried here, James not. But it appears very likely that James is the famous J. S. Neilson, who invented the hot blast furnace that revolutionised the iron industry.

The 'Twomax' Building (former cotton mill), as viewed from the former Gorbals Burial Ground.

25. The 'Twomax' Building - Former Cotton Mill

Return to Old Rutherglen Road. The old industrial buildings opposite, recently converted into offices and studios by a private company, were constructed as a cotton mill over the period 1816-1821. It is the oldest surviving iron-framed, 'fireproof' mill in Glasgow, possibly the oldest in Scotland. The first owner was Robert Humphreys, followed by Robert Thomson, also of Adelphi Cotton Works. It was the subject of industrial disputes in 1824 (when there were two shootings in Ballater Street) and 1837 (when some of Thomson's employees were attacked). Cotton spinning ceased in the 1860s and the mill has more recently been used for the manufacture of clothing, most recently by Twomax (hence the building's familiar name) and W. H. Perkins. On the west side of the main mill building is a vertical array of French doors, originally loading bays served by hoisting apparatus above.

Hutchesontown 'Area A' (Ballater Place) from Old Rutherglen Road.

26. Commercial Road/Ballater Place - Hutchesontown 'Area A'

Retrace your steps for a short distance along Old Rutherglen Road and turn left into Commercial Road. The houses on the right-hand side, through to Ballater Place, were the first to be built in the original redevelopment of Hutchesontown. Dating from 1958, these three and four-storey buildings, designed by the City Architectural and Planning Department, still remain amongst the most attractive in the area. The development received a Saltire Society Housing Design Award and a commendation from the Civic Trust.

Hutchesontown 'Area B', now generally known as 'Riverside'.

27. Commercial Court/Waddell Court - Hutchesontown 'Area B'

To the right, on the opposite side of busy Ballater Street, is the second phase of the Hutchesontown redevelopment, designed by Robert Matthew, Johnson-Marshall & Partners. Dating from 1964 when it also received a Saltire award and a Civic Trust commendation, the scheme is a relatively attractive mixture of multi-storey flats and low rise tenements, all having been recently re-roofed. Further along Commercial Road is the site of the home of Jimmy Stokes who was awarded the Victoria Cross posthumously for his valour during the liberation of Europe in 1945.

28. Blessed John Duns Scotus RC Church

On the near left hand corner of Commercial Road and Ballater Street is the Blessed John Duns Scotus Church, formerly dedicated to St. Luke. It was completed in 1975 and the architect was William J. Gilmour. The exterior features a steep

Corner tower of the Blessed John Duns Scotus Church.

monopitch roof rising to a 'prow-like' tower at the north-west corner, while inside it is simple and impressive. Now the home of the Franciscans, this is now the only Roman Catholic church in the Gorbals, the congregation of the former St. Luke's having been combined with those of St. John's, Laurieston, St. Francis' (see item 23) and St. Bonaventure's, Caledonia Road. Both St. John's and St. Bonaventure's Churches have been demolished, but the bell of St. John's hangs from a small belltower in the church grounds. Here also, in the atrium to the new Greyfriars Centre are kept the relics (bones) of St Valentine and stones from the Medieval and Victorian Franciscan friaries. The present church replaces premises on the ground floor of a dual purpose building immediately to the west which had the associated primary school above (demolished in 1987). An interesting tradition which still continues is the holding of monthly masses in Lithuanian - at one time, there were many Lithuanians in Gorbals, some fleeing from the Czar, some from later enemies, although most of them and their descendants now live in the Motherwell area.

29. Gorbals Leisure Centre

Turn left into Ballater Street (formerly known as Govan Street). On the opposite side, the new Gorbals Leisure Centre is being built by Glasgow City Council. Clad with steel panels and roofed in natural aluminium, this 'high-tech' building will provide the area with an eight lane 25 metre swimming pool, a leisure pool with flume, a sports hall, a tennis hall, a dance studio, health and fitness suites, a creche and a cafe. Midway along the Ballater Street frontage was once situated the 'Coffin Works' - named after its shape, not its product. Here the work was to prepare skins for the furriers - and here the last Glasgow outbreak of the deadly disease anthrax occurred in 1905.

The Ballater Street elevation of the new Gorbals Leisure Centre.

30. Adelphi Centre

Turn right into Florence Street. To the right, behind the new Gorbals Leisure Centre can be seen the Adelphi Centre. Originally built in 1963-66 as a secondary school by architects Boissevain & Osmond, its main classroom block was converted into a training and employment centre in 1997 by Wylie & Court, transforming the exterior from monochrome simplicity to a more colourful 'business park' look.

Below:-The east side of the Adelphi Centre with part of the Glasgow College of Nautical Studies visible in the background.

Opposite:-Ballater Street, looking east, in 1955. On the left, where the road narrows, can be seen the 'Coffin Works'; this side of the street is now occupied by the Gorbals Leisure Centre. The only building on the photograph which still remains is the three-storey building on the right.

This side of Florence Street was the birthplace of local folk hero Benny Lynch (1913-1946), who became World and British Flyweight Boxing Champion. He was born in No 17, one of the many teeming closes that led off Rose Street, as it was then called, and a nearby street, Benny Lynch Court, in the Crown Street development (item 20), has been named after him. Where the car park for the new Gorbals Leisure Centre now sits was Adelphi Sporting Club, a converted brass foundry, where his talents were first discovered by Sammy Wilson, his promoter.

31. Florence Street Clinic

The clinic opposite is important for all Gorbals children. From the mid 19th century, Glasgow, under the leadership of some brilliant and compassionate Medical Officers of Health, fought hard to improve living and health conditions. Before this, infant mortality had been very high. One measure taken at the start of this century was the setting up of clinics where babies and children could not only be treated for their illness, but where the causes of ailments could be studied, and parents helped to avoid them. Florence Street was the fourth of these clinics and was built in 1937.

32. Former Adelphi Terrace Public School

At the end of Florence Street is situated the former Adelphi Terrace Public School, now the Interior Design Annexe of the Glasgow College of Building and Printing. The school was designed by architect T. L. Watson in the Renaissance style, dates from 1894, and has survived unaltered, with original gate pillars and cast-iron railings intact.

The Interior Design Annexe of the Glasgow College of Building and Printing, originally Adelphi Terrace Public School.

The Tidal Weir and Pipe Bridge over the Clyde to Glasgow Green.

33. Tidal Weir and Pipe Bridge
Before turning left along the riverside towards Albert Bridge, you will see the Tidal Weir and Pipe Bridge a short distance upstream. The weir or caul is Scotland's only example of a moveable river-control weir, and marks the upper tidal limit of the River Clyde. Its sluice gates control the flow to give constant water depth upstream, thus preventing erosion of the river banks, and can be raised to allow boats to pass at full tide. The present structure includes handsome, Classical, red ashlar piers and abutments built in 1896-1901 to the design of A. B. McDonald, City Engineer with, on top, two linked parallel bridges, each supporting a service pipe and dating from 1945-49. It replaced a fixed weir and navigation lock constructed in 1852.

34. Albert Bridge
The first river crossing downstream is Albert Bridge, a three-arched cast-iron bridge on stone piers built in 1870-72 by Bell & Miller, Engineers at a cost of £48,900. It was a replacement for earlier structures, firstly Hutchesontown Bridge, built over the period 1794-5 to serve the new suburb on the south bank, followed by another short-lived bridge completed in 1834.

Glasgow College of Nautical Studies from Albert Bridge.

35. Glasgow College of Nautical Studies

Cross Laurieston Road (formerly part of Crown Street) and join the upgraded riverside walkway with the Glasgow College of Nautical Studies on the left. The main college buildings, the subject of a Civic Trust Award, were opened in 1969 by Lord Mountbatten of Burma, the architects being Robert Matthew, Johnson-Marshall & Partners. In *Buildings of Scotland*, the main block is described as "a clean-cut, white-tiled cube with a forest of rooftop radar masts, giving a truly nautical look". There is also a domed planetarium, while over the riverside walkway can be seen an overhead link to the college jetty.

The upgraded walkway along the Gorbals bank of the River Clyde - this is the stretch between the Albert and Victoria Bridges.

The walkway itself is the first phase of landscape work which is gradually extending to the full length of the Gorbals' river frontage. The works are generally traditional in character, incorporating the reproduction Glasgow lampposts noticed in Carlton Place at the beginning of the walk.

36. St. Enoch Bridge

Crossing the walkway and the river is St. Enoch Bridge, a highly decorative replacement for the City of Glasgow Union Railway's original structure of 1864-7. The present five-arch bridge with side spans dates from 1898-1902, was built primarily to serve the new St. Enoch Station, and was designed by the engineer, William Melville. Its most notable features are the red sandstone turrets, both octagonal and square in section.

St. Enoch Bridge with the dome and minaret of the Glasgow Central Mosque just showing against the bulk of the Norfolk Court flats.

37. Glasgow Central Mosque and Islamic Centre

Beyond the railway bridge stands the new Glasgow Mosque, a distinctive building originally designed by W. M. Copeland & Associates and completed in 1984 by the Coleman Ballantine Partnership. The architects described it as a "fusion between Scottish tradition, forms of Islamic building, and the simple logic and economics of modern constructions". Its tall, slender minaret and multi-faceted dome are now familiar City sights and the internal lighting of the dome in the evening is an attractive feature. The mosque, apart from its religious significance, reflects the Gorbals tradition of

The Glasgow Central Mosque and Islamic Centre, as viewed from the south-west.

openness and welcome to people who have come from other countries to Scotland. It has recently been extended to include sports and social/welfare facilities.

38. Victoria Bridge

The next bridge over the Clyde is Victoria Bridge. The current five-arched sandstone structure, encased in Irish granite, cost £46,000 when it was built in 1851-54. It was designed by John Walker from London. It stands on the same site as the original stone Glasgow Bridge erected by Bishop Rae of Glasgow in 1345. Its wooden predecessor was associated with William Wallace in his struggle for Scottish independence. On one occasion, in 1297, it is said that Wallace and his men crossed the bridge after attacking the Bishop's Castle and defeating the English at the Battle of the Bell of the Brae. Tradition has it that, after the battle, many of the defeated English finished up in the Stock Well, close by the bridge.

39. Sheriff Courthouse

On the opposite side of Gorbals Street, the Sheriff Courthouse "stands as aloof as a fortress" in its landscaped, riverside setting. Dating from 1980-86, it is reputed to be the second largest in Europe and contains 21 courtrooms. The architects were Keppie Henderson & Partners. The exterior is faced with sandstone and Danish marble; while a striking feature of the interior is a top-lit gallery along the spine, overlooked by access balconies and crossed by glass and metal bridges.

To complete the walk, cross Gorbals Street and pass along the court's terrace to return to Carlton Place and the walk's starting point at the suspension bridge. Alternatively, walkers may wish to follow the second offshoot from the main walk which explores the site of the original Gorbals village.

SECOND OFFSHOOT FROM MAIN ROUTE

At Victoria Bridge, turn left into Gorbals Street. This was the Main Street of the old Gorbals village, leading south from the medieval Glasgow Bridge. Before the 19th Century, it was a village of hand-loom weavers, maltmen (brewers in a small way), agricultural workers, barrelmakers and gunsmiths. You can see the work of one family of gunsmiths - the Manns - in the Art Gallery and Museum, Kelvingrove. The coming of the cotton mills and the early stages of the Industrial Revolution, combined with an influx of people seeking work, caused the old village to burst its seams and become a disease-ridden maze of overcrowding, with houses and workshops set up wherever there were a few feet of space. Gradually this was cleared and in the 1870s, Main Street was widened, straightened and lined with tenements by the City Improvement Trust. All of these disappeared in the 1970s except the bank tenement on the right in the distance (item J).

The site of the Mosque and Islamic Centre was formerly occupied by sandstone tenements and the second oldest distillery in Glasgow. Before that was an orchard sloping down to the river, and a few tenements of two or three-storey houses with long gardens behind, built in the late 17th or early 18th Century. Before them, stretching southwards as far as the Citizen's Theatre, and as far east as the Nautical College, was a tract of land called St Ninian's Croft, belonging to the Bishop of Glasgow. This land housed Glasgow's leper hospital, grew its food, earned its money by being let out in portions and provided its church and burial ground.

Gorbals Cross around 1910, with tenements designed by Alexander 'Greek' Thomson in the background. The clock tower and public drinking fountain reflected its role as an important local focal point; now the same view is over a busy road junction towards the Sheriff Courthouse (City Archives).

Where the Sheriff Courthouse now stands were more tenements built between 1871 and 1891 to replace the crumbling, crowded vennels of the old village. Facing the river were David Hamilton's Gorbals Parish or John Knox Church (1810-1974) with its beautiful spire, once an outstanding riverside landmark, and Buchan Street School, the direct descendant of the Old Parish School of Gorbals. Buchan Street School was built on the site of the 'Wheatsheaf Inn' one of the fashionable inns of the City, with stables, dining rooms, concert rooms and assembly rooms for dances. In this vicinity also was Glasgow's first distillery, begun in 1786 by Mr William Menzies. His licence was the fourth to be granted in Scotland.

G. Gorbals Cross

The busy crossroads ahead was once the focal point of the area. It now takes a lot of imagination to visualise the sense of enclosure once given by the surrounding four-storey tenements (those on the north-west corner were designed by Alexander 'Greek' Thomson), busy with commercial activity on the ground floor. For many years, there was a central clock tower, and the last survivor in 1975 was the gentlemen's public lavatory with its green railings, also in the middle of the road.

Cross Ballater Street and pass the Legal Centre which, on its corner site, makes a forlorn contribution to restoring the former sense of enclosure. Where a pend leads through to the car park behind was once the junction of Rutherglen Loan, the start of the road to Rutherglen. Prior to 1869, this street corner was occupied by the former St Ninian's Chapel, founded in connection with the leper hospital in 1494.

Immediately to the north was the Elphinstone Tower - a town mansion house with a tower and four turrets which gave it a castellated appearance. This was erected around the beginning of the 17th Century by Sir George Elphinstone, who fell heavily into debt before he could finish it. The mansion house originally occupied two sides of a courtyard, with the tower on the west side. After Glasgow Town Council took possession of the group of buildings in 1650, they were let to a variety of tenants, then the tower became a prison and the former chapel used as the courthouse and parish school. In 1808 the chapel was converted into the local police headquarters and continued to function as such until 1827 when the buildings were sold, converted into shops, flats and a pub, and started to fall into disrepair. The former mansion house was demolished by 1848, but the tower and chapel survived for another twenty years, the tower being partially dismantled and finishing up ignominiously as a ragstore.

A short distance eastwards along Rutherglen Loan, a corner tenement at Muirhead Street (later known as Inverkip Street) was the birthplace of Allan Pinkerton, the founder of the well-known American detective agency which bears his name. The agency's trademark of an open eye was the source of the term 'private eye'.

Gorbals Street, looking north, in 1965, before the second wave of clearance. On the right can be seen the original frontage of the Citizens' Theatre.

Today's view of the street frontage shown opposite with the Citizens' Theatre in the foreground and the Legal Centre stretching away to Gorbals Cross.

H. The Citizen's Theatre

Next on the left is the Citizens' Theatre of international theatrical renown, given a new brick facade and foyer by the Building Design Partnership in 1989 at the same time as the construction of the Legal Centre. For several years prior to that date, it had an unsightly, truncated external appearance which must have come as a considerable shock to many first-time visitors, but, before the fateful 1970s, it had an imposing front with columns topped by six allegorical figures. This had originally been the facade of the Union Bank in Ingram Street - when the bank was altered, the far-seeing builder of the tenements on either side of the theatre bought the columns, and the architect James Sellars incorporated them into the new buildings. With the demolition of the tenements, the facade went too - although at least Mossman's statues were preserved and are now displayed behind the present first floor glazing. But it is a jewel box of colour, decoration and brilliance inside, with two horseshoe tiers on cast-iron columns, originally built in 1878 by Campbell Douglas. Before the theatre became the Citizens', it was the Royal Princess Theatre, famous for its pantomime.

I. Well and Rose Garden

On the opposite side of the street is a small rose demonstration garden. At its entrance is a red sandstone well which was relocated in 1989 from its original site at the corner of Crown Street and Cathcart Road, in front of the former St. Ninian's Wynd Church. The carved relief panels, reflecting local history and culture, were added by Jim Harvey, then a student at Glasgow School of Art.

J. Tenement - 162-170 Gorbals Street
Beyond the rose garden is a lone four-storey tenement, constructed in red ashlar. This remnant of the old Gorbals dates from 1900 and was designed by Salmon, Son & Gillespie in the Glasgow Style. The ground floor contained a banking hall (British Linen) and a shop unit. Return to Victoria Bridge and rejoin the main route to the starting point of the walk.

POSTCRIPT

The Heritage Walk entered Laurieston by one suspension bridge and the first offshoot from the main route visited another at the north-east corner of Hutchesontown. Between them are many of Glasgow's major old bridges and the tidal weir which reminds us how far people have engineered even the river. It gives cause for reflection that while the Gorbals was once known as Brig-end, many beginnings were also made in the area - in the lives of fugitives from poverty or danger, in town planning and in industry. The area has since seen many changes, not all for the better, but throughout, the people of the Gorbals have felt a never ceasing pride in their community.

Right:- At the end of the Heritage Walk, the suspension bridge at Carlton Place takes visitors back to the city centre.

REFERENCES

'An ABC of the Gorbals', Gorbals History Research Group, Glasgow, 1996.

'City of the Dead' edited by Charlotte Hutt, City Libraries and Archives, Glasgow, 1996.

'Exodus from the Brave New Gorbals' by William Hill, *The Scotsman*, 18th September 1979.

'Glasgow 1990' by Campbell R. Steven, *Scottish Field*, March 1964.

'Glasgow Jewry: A Guide to the History and Community of the Jews in Glasgow' by Dr. Kenneth E. Collins, Scottish Jewish Archives Committee, 1993.

'Glasgow Past and Present' by Senex, Second Edition, David Robertson & Co., Glasgow, 1884.

'Gorbals - An Illustrated History' by Eric Eunson, Richard Stenlake Publishing, Ochiltree, 1996.

'Gorbals Annual Report and Strategic Framework 1997', Gorbals Officer Working Group, 1997.

'Gorbals Local Plan - Survey Report', City of Glasgow District Council, 1984.

'Gorbals Local Plan - Written Statement', City of Glasgow District Council, 1994.

'Hutchesontown Housing Development - Bright Modern Flats Replace Slums', *The Scotsman*, 24th August 1972.

'Hutchesontown/Part Gorbals Comprehensive Development Area, 1956 - Survey Report, Corporation of the City of Glasgow, 1956.

'Hutchesontown/Part Gorbals Comprehensive Development Area, 1956 - Written Statement', Corporation of the City of Glasgow, 1956.

'Industry on the Move', Corporation of Glasgow, January 1959.

'Laurieston/Gorbals Comprehensive Development Area, 1965 - Survey Report', Corporation of the City of Glasgow, 1965.

'Laurieston/Gorbals Comprehensive Development Area, 1965 - Written Statement', Corporation of the City of Glasgow, 1965.

'Miracle in the Gorbals' by Ninian Johnston, *Architectural Prospect*, Spring 1957.

'Proposals for Comprehensive Redevelopment - Report to the Housing and Planning Committees', Corporation of the City of Glasgow, 1953.

'Queen Elizabeth Square: The Future', Report to City of Glasgow District Council by the Director of Housing, July 1990.

'Rebuilding Scotland - The Postwar Vision 1945-1975' edited by Miles Glendinning, Tuckwell Press, East Linton, 1997.

'St Francis Centre' by Anthony ODoibhailein, Gorbals History Research Group, Glasgow, 1998.

'The Buildings of Scotland - Glasgow' by Elizabeth Williamson, Anne Riches & Malcolm Higgs, Penguin Books, London, 1990.

'The City that Disappeared - Glasgow's Demolished Architecture' by Frank Worsdall, Molendinar Press, 1981.

'The Statistical Account of Scotland - Volume Fifth' by Sir John Sinclair, Edinburgh, 1793 (Parish of the Gorbals of Glasgow by the Rev. Mr. William Anderson).

'Third Time Lucky? The History and Hopes of the Gorbals', Gorbals History Research Group, Glasgow.

FURTHER RECOMMENDED READING

'From Small Acorns', edited by Sandra Wilson and Alan Dunlop, Gorbals Umbrella Group/Glasgow Institute of Architects, Park Circus Promotions, Glasgow, 1997.
'Back to the Future... - The Gorbals Community Report' by Gorbals Research and Information Team (True GRIT), Glasgow, 1997.
'Gorbals Community Directory' by Maryanna Robinson, The Gorbals Umbrella Group, Glasgow, 1997.
'Architecture of Glasgow' by Gomme and Walker, Lund Humphries, 1987.
'The Life and Work of Alexander Thomson' by Ronald McFadzean, Routledge & Kegan Paul, London, 1979.
'"Greek" Thomson' edited by Gavin Stamp and Sam McKinstry, Edinburgh University Press, 1994.

ARCHITECTURAL GLOSSARY

An attempt has been made to avoid the use of architectural jargon in this guide, but where technical terms have been unavoidable, their definitions are set out below.

Art Deco: Style of decorative art characteristic of the 1920s and 1930s, subsequent to Art Nouveau.

Ashlar: Masonry of large blocks with even faces and square edges.

Cupola: Small domed turret crowning a roof.

Glasgow Style: Variations of Art Nouveau peculiar to certain Glasgow architects around the year 1900.

Pavilion: Projecting subdivision of large building, forming an angle feature in the centre of the main facade or a large end block.

Portico: Porch with detached columns.

Rotunda: Building or structure circular in plan.

ACKNOWLEDGEMENTS

This book has been revised, updated and extended by Ronald Smith of Development and Regeneration Services, Glasgow City Council, with the willing co-operation of the original authors, Charlotte Hutt and Ellen McAllister. The authors would particularly like to thank Iain Paterson, David Horner, Colin Mackie, Maureen Lanigan, Sam McCall and Margaret McBride for contributions of their expertise.

All of the photographs, illustrations and maps, except where otherwise credited, have been derived from archive material held by Development and Regeneration Services. Where applicable, every effort has been made to secure permission to include material in this book; in this connection, the assistance of Glasgow Libraries and Archives was appreciated. The publisher apologises for any errors or significant omissions and would be grateful to be notified of any corrections.

Printed by Glasgow City Council Printworks.

THE GORBALS

Map showing the layout of the area and the route of the Heritage Walk

Number	Place of Interest	Listed Building Category
1.	Carlton Suspension Bridge	A
2.	Carlton Place	A & B
3.	Laurieston House	A
4.	South Portland Street	
5.	21-25 Carlton Court - Former Stables	B
6.	Cumbrae House	B
7.	20-22 Bridge St - Former Commercial Bank	B
8.	Bridge Street Station	B
9.	63-67 Bridge Street - Former Savings Bank	B
10.	144-150 Norfolk Street/69-71 Bridge Street	B
11.	The Coliseum	B
12.	The 'New' Bedford	B
13.	Railway Arches	
14.	Birthplace of Sir Hugh Roberton	
15.	Former Eglinton Congregational Church	B
16.	Former Abbotsford Primary School	B
17.	St Andrew's Works	B
18.	Former Chalmers Free Church	B
19.	Caledonia Road Church	A
20.	Crown Street Regeneration Project	
21.	Blackfriars Primary School	
22.	Hutchesontown 'Area D' - Scottish Special Housing Association	
23.	St. Francis' Centre and Former Friary	A
24.	Gorbals Burial Ground	
25.	The 'Twomax' Building - Former Cotton Mill	B
26.	Commercial Road/Ballater Place - Hutchesontown 'Area A'	
27.	Commercial Court/Waddell Court - Hutchesontown 'Area B'	
28.	Blessed John Duns Scotus RC Church	
29.	Gorbals Leisure Centre	
30.	Adelphi Centre	
31.	Florence Street Clinic	
32.	Former Adelphi Terrace Public School	B
33.	Tidal Weir and Pipe Bridge	B
34.	Albert Bridge	B
35.	Glasgow College of Nautical Studies	
36.	St. Enoch Bridge	B
37.	Glasgow Central Mosque and Islamic Centre	
38.	Victoria Bridge	B
39.	Sheriff Courthouse	

Offshoots from main route ▪▪▪▪▪

Letter	Place of Interest	Listed Building Category
A.	Gatehouse to the Southern Necropolis	B
B.	The Southern Necropolis	
C.	Dixon's Blazes	
D.	Former Hutchesontown District Library	C
E.	Gorbals East Renewal Area - New Housing	
F.	St. Andrew's Suspension Bridge	A
G.	Gorbals Cross	
H.	The Citizens' Theatre	B
I.	Well and Rose Garden	
J.	Tenement - 162-170 Gorbals Street	A

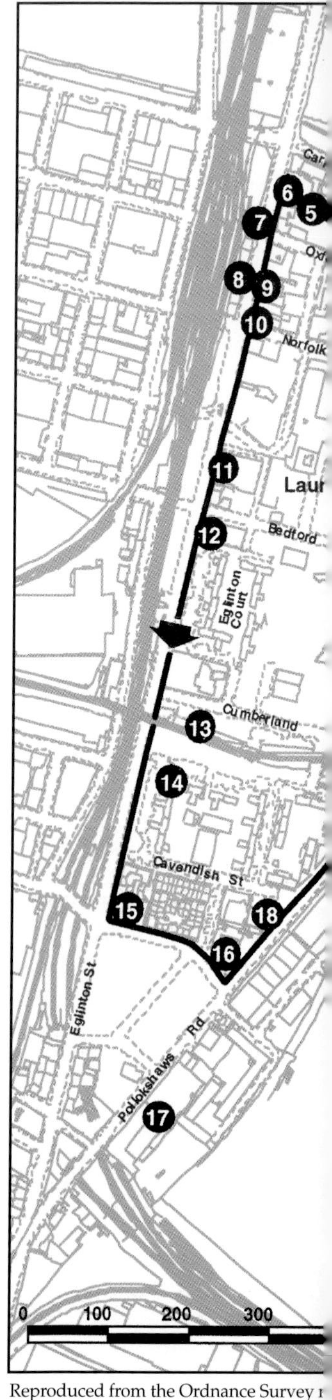

Reproduced from the Ordnance Survey r
infringes Crown Copyright and may lea

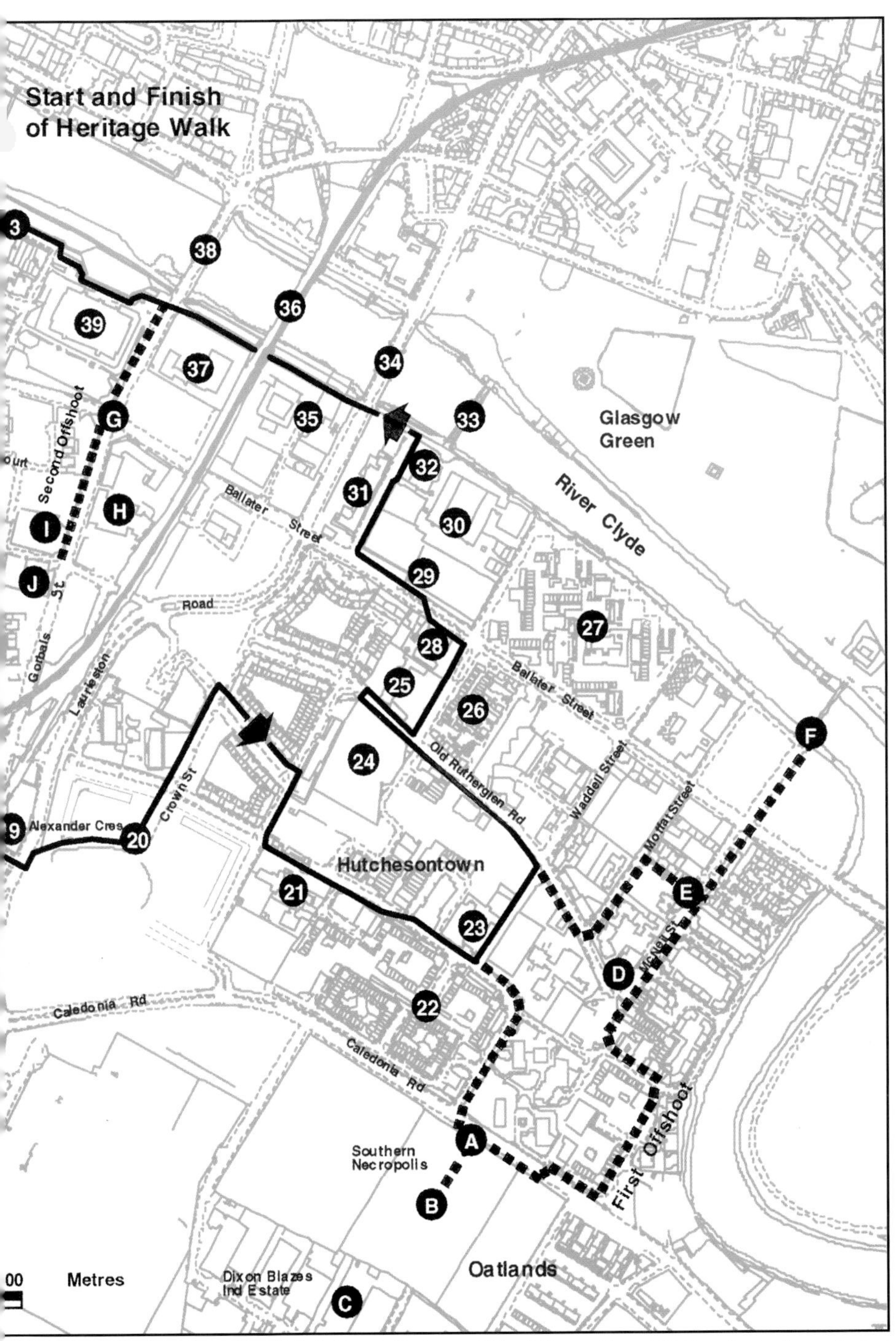

Start and Finish of Heritage Walk
Glasgow Green
River Clyde
Ballater Street
Road
Gorbals St
Laurieston
Second Offshoot
Crown St
Alexander Cres
Old Rutherglen Rd
Waddell Street
Moffat Street
McNeil St
Hutchesontown
Caledonia Rd
Southern Necropolis
First Offshoot
Oatlands
Dixon Blazes Ind Estate
Metres